THE TANTRIC RITE

ARYA AETERNA

Book II

THE TANTRIC RITE

Arya Aeterna Book II

Published by Sanctus Arya Press

First edition, published in October of 2025 by Sanctus Arya Press.

Paperback: 978-1-968394-02-8

Hardcover: 978-1-968394-03-5

Library of Congress Number pending.

Cover art, editing, layout, and *yantra* (p. 8) by Frater Sigma.

Concluding illustration taken from the public domain.

More at:

aryaaeterna.com

sanctusarya.com

This volume was crafted by anonymous initiates in service to the Great Work and furthering a Northern Esoteric Tradition of Perennial Wisdom.

ॐ त्र्यंबकं यजामहे सुगंधिं पुष्टिवर्धनम्।

उर्वारुकमिव बन्धनान् मृत्योर्मुक्षीय माऽमृतात्॥

Om Tryambakaṃ yajāmahe sugandhiṃ puṣṭi-vardhanam
urvārukam iva bandhanān mṛtyor mukṣīya mā'mṛtāt

"We worship the Three-Eyed One (Shiva), who is fragrant and who nourishes all beings. May He liberate us from the bondage of death, like the ripe cucumber is freed from the vine, but not from immortality."

—Ṛigveda

Table of Contents

Introduction

Modernity, as critiqued by Julius Evola in *Ride the Tiger*, represents a profound spiritual crisis: a descent into a profane world where traditional frameworks of meaning have eroded. The triumph of rationalist materialism has severed humanity's connection to transcendence, leaving what Evola called the "*differentiated man*," attuned to higher metaphysical realities, stranded in a wasteland of cynicism.

As a path to navigate this crisis, this exposition offers a practical, contemporary Tantric practice rooted in Evola's Radical Tradition and Magical Idealism. Tantra, with its emphasis on transformative ritual, sacred sexuality, and harnessing divine energy (Shakti), offers a dynamic means of transcendence for a differentiated man, aligning with Evola's call to *ride the tiger* of modern chaos while remaining anchored in an upright, ordered bearing.

Drawing upon Evola and others, this work emphasizes the symbolic potency of Tantric language, centrality of erotic union as a ritual of polarity, and awakening of *kundalinī* as means of surpassing nihilism. The approach offers a necessary antidote to the spiritual desolation in our age by incorporating an ethos of will-to-power rooted in sacred masculinity.

René Guénon first diagnosed modernity as a state of spiritual degeneration marked by the loss of sacred hierarchies and metaphysical cornerstones. He describes the "*Kali Yuga*" as a final age of cosmic decline where material concerns dominate and spiritual authority is replaced by secular ideologies.

For Evola, this manifests as a dissolution of the heroic, hierarchical values of Tradition, leaving an individual adrift in a world of relativism and chaos. The differentiated man, however, is not bound by this decay. As articulated in *Ride the Tiger*, such an individual must strategically engage with the modern world, using its forces as a catalyst for superiority rather than succumbing to despair.

Tantra, particularly as elucidated in Evola's *Yoga of Power*, emerges as a uniquely suited path for this task. Unlike exoteric religious systems often demanding passive adherence, Tantra is an initiatic tradition requiring active participation in the transformation of self. Its esoteric nature aligns with Mircea Eliade's concept of the sacred as a lived experience accessible through ritual, and symbol.

Tantra's emphasis on the body, energy, and polarity makes it an applicable basis for one to exploit modernity's unruly force as a source of potency. Its relevance is further emphasized in its understanding of *"world as power"* — a vision of reality as a dynamic interplay of Shiva (consciousness) and Shakti (energy) that can be directly engaged through operative interaction.

Tantra is not simply a metaphysical system; it is a firsthand, empirical path effectively integrating theoretical and practical.

Its language is symbolic and encoded in layers of meaning that reveal themselves through disciplined practice. As Eliade notes in *Yoga: Immortality and Freedom*, Tantric rituals are designed to awaken a practitioner to the divine within and without.

For Evola, this aligns with Magical Idealism, a doctrine that reality is shaped by the will of an awakened individual. The differentiated man becomes a co-creator of reality via Tantric practice, transcending the profane world's limitations.

The initiatic nature of Tantra requires a radical commitment to self-transformation. Evola's concept of *riding the tiger* serves as a guiding metaphor. A seeker does not reject the modern world but engages it as a field of action, using its trials to fuel spiritual ascent.

This approach resonates with Friedrich Nietzsche's call to affirm life in the face of nihilism, reinterpreted through a Tantric lens of destruction and creation. As destroyer of illusion Shiva embodies a radical detachment necessary to exceed false values. Shakti, a creative force, provides energy for this task.

At the heart of Tantric practice lies a ritual of erotic union, described as a means of transcending the mundane through an integration of masculine and feminine principles. In *Yoga of Power*, Evola emphasizes an ontological significance of gender polarity wherein male (Shiva, consciousness) and female (Shakti, energy) are cosmic forces far surpassing mere biology.

The ritual of *Maithuna* (sacred union) transforms physical intimacy into a spiritual act, aligning practitioners with divine polarities underlying existence. This practice is anti-hedonistic and highly disciplined, requiring mastery over desire. As Sir John Woodroffe (Arthur Avalon) explains, the objective is not indulgence but a sublimation of sexual energy into power.

Intercourse becomes a microcosm for an ontological pairing of Shiva and Shakti; opposites are reconciled and practitioners glimpse a unified reality beyond form. For a differentiated man this offers a way beyond nihilism, as the undertaking affirms life while exceeding material limitations.

In practical terms, sacred sexuality requires preparation and intentionality. Partners must approach the ritual with shared reverence, grounding their practice in awareness, breathwork, and visualization. The physical act is secondary to an energetic exchange: practitioners awaken and channel *kundalinī*, a latent energy at the base of the spine. This aligns with an emphasis on discipline and detachment, ensuring sex remains a means of transcendence rather than descent into sensuality.

An awakening of *kundalinī*, described by Woodroffe as the "*Serpent Power*," is central to Tantric practice. This coiled energy represents Shakti's raw potential as a divine feminine force. Through methodical practice (yoga, ascesis, mantra, ritual) one activates this energy, guiding it to unite with Shiva at the crown, achieving a state of transcendence.

Practically, *kundalinī* awakening begins with foundational exercises: *pranayama* (breath control) to stabilize energy and *asana* (postures) to purify the body. Mantras such as *bija* (seed) sounds associated with each *chakra* (energy center) amplify a practitioner's connection to cosmic forces.

For example, chanting "*LAM*" while fixating at the *muladhara chakra* grounds a practitioner. Meanwhile, "*OM*" directed at the *sahasrara chakra* prompts unity with the divine. These actions align an individual with the *world as power*, where every deed evokes creation and destruction alike.

The hazards of *kundalinī* awakening (as cautioned by both Evola and Woodroffe) seem to dictate either careful guidance from a guru or a thorough understanding of a tradition. Without proper preparation, one risks psycho-physiological imbalance. However, for a differentiated man this risk is part of one's heroic path: a confrontation with the abyss echoing a call to *live dangerously*.

To implement a Tantric practice in the modern world, one must incorporate higher principles into daily discipline. Study sacred texts to grasp Traditional symbolism and metaphysics. Establish a routine of pranayama and asana to prepare the body and mind. Focus on aligning the chakras through visualization and mantra.

If practicing with a partner, approach sacred sexuality with reverence, using breathwork, visualization, and other processes to build energy and sacralize the act. Solo practitioners can work with internal polarity through contemplation on Shiva-Shakti.

Apply Evola's idea of *riding the tiger* by using modernity's challenges — stress, distraction, temptation — as opportunities for detachment and focus. Transform mundane activities into acts of mindfulness through deliberate denial or permission.

Seek a community or teacher rooted in authentic tradition to avoid the pitfalls of superficial New Age or other subversive, pseudo-religious interpretations. If no mentor is available, rely on rigorous study and discernment.

The crisis of modernity demands a drastic response. With its emphasis on sacred sexuality, *kundalinī* awakening, and balance of opposites, Tantra offers a path for differentiated men to reroute the modern world's dross while pursuing a higher course of life.

By harnessing the fire of Shakti and aligning with timeless principles of Tradition, one transforms the despair of present-day existence into grounds for spiritual opportunity. This path — both practical and philosophical — embodies an ethos of creation through destruction, offering a way to immanentize the eternal.

Metaphysical Foundations of Tantra

Tantra, often misunderstood in its modern appropriations, stands as one of the most potent expressions of an ancient Indo-Aryan metaphysical worldview. Far from being a degenerate cult of sensualism, its roots are deeply embedded in Vedic Tradition, reflecting a spiritual grammar both vital and transcendent. From this elevated perspective Tantra reveals itself not merely as a path among many, but as a discipline of spiritual virility and sovereignty structured upon principles of ontological realism, inner transformation, and sacred intimacy.

At its foundation, Tantra does not represent a deviation from Vedic *dharma* but an intensification of its esoteric and initiatic essence. Where exoteric Vedism privileges cosmic order (*ṛta*) and sacrificial continuity, Tantra emphasizes mastery over becoming (*saṃsāra*) through direct engagement with power (*śakti*) in its raw and immanent form. It is not antinomian in the modern, nihilistic sense, but rather *metanomian*: it transcends law by internalizing it.

Guénon places *Vedānta* as a doctrinal summit; Tantra, while engaging with the same metaphysical truths, directs attention to the ontological mechanics of transformation. It entails how

Absolute (*Ātman*) reflects in *prakṛti*, and consciousness can be made operative through yogic and ritual technologies. In this, Tantra preserves a primordial Indo-European initiatic mode similar to Iranian and Hellenic warrior-ascetics — knowledge was not distinct from power and both were linked to being.

In *Yoga: Immortality and Freedom,* Mircea Eliade attests to the archaic spiritual ethos pervading Tantric systems. It is the yogin as one who defies death by integrating his being with the eternal. Here we find the essence of Tantric metaphysics: a refusal to be carried along by the flux of becoming and instead use vital power to stand against an involutionary current.

The foundational metaphysical polarity in Tantra is a dual principle of *Śiva* and *Śakti* — the still and dynamic, the Absolute and its Power, awareness and energy. This polarity maps onto a series of binary correspondences: *Puruṣa/Prakṛti*, *Vajra/Padma*, *Idā/Piṅgalā*, Sun/Moon, etc. These dyads are ontological pairs: modes through which the Monad expresses itself in twofold manifestation.

Śiva is pure consciousness (*cit*), formless, unmanifest, and transcendent; *Śakti* is the dynamic principle, *māyā-śakti*, the creative potency that makes manifestation possible. Tantra teaches that liberation is not a rejection of *Śakti*, but rather the full integration of her power into awareness, leading to their union (*yāmala*) in an adept. This is not a symbolic union but an ontological realization — a reversal of metaphysical exile and return to the ground of Being through active mastery over a world of energies.

This polarity unfolds into the *tattvas*: categories of reality representing a descent of the Absolute into manifestation. From *Śiva-tattva* to the lowest elements (*bhūtas*), these principles delineate a structure of reality, allowing a practitioner to ascend back through them via *sādhanā*. Likewise, the three *guṇas* — *sattva, rajas, tamas* — are modes of energy, and their power shapes both cosmological processes and human temperaments (*divya*, *vīra*, *pāśu*). The Tantric path, particularly through Evola's lens, valorizes a *vīra* type: a warrior-sage whose orientation is conquest — not primarily of an external world, but instead of self, becoming, and illusion.

The Tantric worldview affirms a multi-tiered cosmos: the *lokas* or worlds, arranged from gross to subtle, from *bhū-loka* (physical) to *satya-loka* (realm of truth). These are not symbols, but planes of existence populated by sentient life and organized according to karma and levels of emanation. The adept seeks to surpass or at least dominate all of these worlds and beings not by denial, but integrating and mastering their influences.

In Tantric terms *Ātman* is both immanent and transcendent — present within the heart (*hṛdaya*), yet identical with Brahman, the unconditioned Absolute. This doctrine is crucial: one does not attain the Absolute outside oneself, but through activating and elevating it in one's self via disciplined action and spiritual transformation. Guénon's affirmation of *Ātman* as central to human realization is complemented in Tantra by concrete techniques to make this realization operative.

Yoga, particularly as approached by Tantra, is an ascesis of power (*tapas*) and willful increase of being. Evola emphasizes in

The Yoga of Power that such practice aims at achieving *icchā-śuddhi* — a purification and concentration of will whereby desire ceases to be scattered and becomes verticalized. Through this, an adept approaches *samyama*: intellectual intuition, a super-conscious concentration that permits identification with the object of knowledge.

Central to Evola's metaphysical reading of Tantra is the doctrine of Magical Idealism positing that consciousness is not passive, but causative. In this view, reality is shaped by the quality and strength of consciousness. This is not solipsism in its basic understanding, but rather an assertion that will aligned with awareness has substantive consequences, especially when charged with vital energy.

In the Tantric context, *kriyā* (action) is not mechanical or ethical activity, but intentional operation whereby techniques like ritual, mantra, and visualization modify the inner and outer cosmos. Through these acts an adept exerts control over subtle forces, bending materiality to the higher authority of spirit. Such feats are grounded in knowledge (*jñāna*), directed by will (*icchā*), and magnified with power (*śakti*).

The false duality of enjoyment and renunciation prevalent in both modern hedonism and reactionary asceticism is overcome in the Tantric method. Enjoyment (*bhoga*) is not shunned, but spiritualized; renunciation is not negation, but interiorization. This is the essence of a *"Tantric Method"* — to affirm the world neither as absolute or illusory, but a potently supple domain to be transfigured at will.

The true Tantric practitioner does not simply contemplate doctrines, but enacts them. The method requires precise ritual action, introspective immersion, and psycho-spiritual discipline. The body, breath, and mind become instruments of ascent.

Kundalinī is often misrepresented as mere physical energy or vital power. However, it must be interpreted as a vehicle for awakening: the Fire of Spirit. It is a potent vertical force that leads to immanent union with a transcendent Self.

This path requires emotional detachment (*vairāgya*) and inner renunciation (*tyāga*) — not world-denial, but its mastery. One must strip away conditioning (*saṃskāras*) and become capable of standing alone. This is an incomparable sovereignty attributed solely to Aryo-Tantric man.

It is not a moral path, but an ontological one. It deals with actuality, not orthodoxy. Hence, Tantra demands an elite type capable of holding tension between opposites (self-denial and affirmation, rigor and enjoyment, dispassion and engagement) without succumbing to confusion, error, or cynicism.

The heart (*hṛdaya*) becomes a center of realization. Through stages of *samyama* or coordinated practice (*dhāraṇā*, *dhyāna*, and *samādhi*) the seeker arrives at a place where thought, will, and being converge. This is an apex of Tantric realization: not fusion with the formless void, but lucid identification with a suprapersonal center: pure subjectivity beyond designation.

Tantra properly understood stands as a radical counterpoint to the atheist-materialism of modernity. Where average men are fragmented, exteriorized, and spiritually inert, the Tantric path affirms a primacy of inner mutation, possibility of metaphysical freedom, and reality of hierarchical being.

For a contemporary seeker frustrated with dead ideologies and pseudo-religious simulacra, Tantra offers not consolation but power. This is foremost expressed as an ability to dominate oneself, reforging individuality into a manifestation of spiritual potency that in turn alters reality in service to a higher self.

Radical Tradition and the Tantric Warrior

When sacred order is eclipsed and all forms are degraded, the only viable orientation for a spiritually awakened individual is toward Radical Tradition. This is not "tradition" as calcified formality or wistful archaism, but Tradition in its metaphysical, primordial sense: a set of superior principles rooted in Being itself. It is a perpetual directive (*sanātana dharma*) that orders civilizations hierarchically, aligns man with a higher authority, and provides a vertical axis of liberation.

Within this context, Tantra offers a specific and forceful mode of spiritual realization. Unlike exoteric religious systems which may tend toward devotional or moral frameworks, Tantra — especially in its *Shaivite-Kaula* currents — engages the world as a field for inner conquest. Here emerges the archetype of a Tantric Warrior: one who embodies the dharma of a *Kṣatriya*, not merely as a caste or function, but an existential stance in defiance of spiritual entropy. This standard is exemplified and championed in Evola's works, especially *Ride the Tiger*, which envisions the man of Tradition as one who stands upright amid the ruins — not to preserve them, but surpass them.

To speak of Radical Tradition is to entreat a revolt — not necessarily as a reactionary conservatism, but an initiation into supra-human principles. Drawing from Guénon's foundations in *Introduction to the Study of the Hindu Doctrines*, Evola asserts that modernity is characterized by inversion: sabotage of higher by lower, elevation of quantity over quality, and denial of the transcendent dimension of existence.

Radical Tradition demands a reversal of this process within the self. This is a return to an inner order of Being that exceeds both collectivist dogmas and individualist illusions. It posits truth is not discovered in external consensus, but in vertical integration with the Real.

In the Hindu world, this is seen in a distinction between *pravṛtti* (the outward path) and *nivṛtti* (a return to the Source). Tantra synthesizes these: it affirms life insofar as it acts as a means for transcendence. Hence, the Tantric warrior is one who engages the world without being "of" it — a theme central to Evola's revised stance on modernity conveyed in *Ride the Tiger*.

The Tantric Warrior and Kṣatriya Ideal

The Tantric practitioner is not a monk, but a householder ascetic. He is a yogi who disciplines power (*śakti*) rather than fleeing from it. In the *Bhagavad Gītā* this archetype is Krishna's ideal: Arjuna, a warrior who conquers not by withdrawal, but perfect action without regard for its result. Krishna instructs Arjuna to act in accordance with his *svadharma*, his essential law, while renouncing desire — *kriyā* without *kāma*.

Guénon's *Studies in Hinduism* (particularly the chapter "Atma-Gītā") affirms the same doctrine: that Self is a silent witness and unmovable axis around which action may revolve without ensnaring the spirit. Evola adapts this for the modern world, contrasting men of Tradition with a degenerate "Animal Ideal" — man immersed in instincts, passions, and a horizontal existence rooted to the earth and ensnared in its cycles.

In Evola's critique, especially in *Ride the Tiger*, the Tantric warrior rises above dual illusions of atheistic materialism and sentimental spiritualism. He acts with precision, without hope or fear, rewards or regrets. His mastery is ontological; he does not seek "happiness" but awakening.

Navigating Modernity with Detached Presence

Evola repeatedly states that in a world where one cannot live as in traditional civilizations, one must learn to "ride the tiger" — master modernity's chaos from within, turning its dissolution into a spiritual challenge. For a Tantric warrior this does not imply adaptation or forfeit, but a higher form of engagement: lucid detachment born of inner stability.

The world is now dominated by nihilism, which Evola identifies with the spiritual exhaustion of Western civilization and disintegration of objective values. He draws parallels with the *Übermensch* as a figure of re-transvaluation; but where Nietzsche ends in ambiguity, we proceed further. A Tantric warrior does not create values *ex nihilo*, but reawakens the primordial order within himself through discipline (*sādhana*), inner fire (*tapas*), and metaphysical grounding (*dharma*).

This detached strength is crucial in relations between the sexes. Evola rejects both romantic sentimentalism and libertine degeneration. In a Tantric context woman is not an object of pleasure nor mundane companion, but Shakti embodied. She personifies a force that can either entrap or liberate based on one's willpower and spiritual orientation.

A Tantric warrior engages the feminine not in domination or submission, but ritualized polarity: an interaction between *Śiva* and *Śakti* where masculine stillness draws forth energy and transmutes it. As in the *Kaula* ritual, this union is a sacrament, not an indulgence. It is an alchemical transmutation whereby duality is overcome along with petty morality.

Sādhana as Inner Discipline and Soteriological Technology

The practical foundation of a Tantric warrior's path is *sadhana*: a regular (often daily), structured routine of exercises aimed at self-overcoming and orientation toward the Absolute. *Sādhana* is not arbitrary; it is a science of inner transformation rooted in metaphysical correspondences and supported by a strict, formal transmission.

This incorporates recitation (*mantra*), breathing techniques (*prāṇāyāma*), visualization (*yantra nyāsa*), ritual (*puja*), and sexual transmutation (*maithuna*). What connects these is not form, but intentionality: to rouse energy, purify intention, and elevate awareness. Evola refers to this as "*Dionysian Apollonism*" — a fusion of ecstatic force with Olympian control.

In Tantra, *Śiva* represents the Apollonian pole: unchanging, self-luminous consciousness. *Śakti* is the Dionysian force: wild, creative, and dissolving. The warrior must neither repress nor indulge the Dionysian, but master it through a solar will. This reflects how power subdued and sanctified fuels transcendence. Without rule it remains chaotic; yet without potency all is sterile.

Acting Without Desire: Causal Law and Liberation

One of the crucial metaphysical insights in *Ride the Tiger* is Evola's treatment of causal law. Echoing the *Gītā* and Vedantic metaphysics, he proposes liberation arises not from passivity, but detached action. This is action exempt from karmic bonds because it is performed absent affinity, desire, or expectation.

This doctrine is quintessentially Tantric. In *Vīra sādhana*, the adept may engage in acts traditionally forbidden (consuming meat or wine and having sex), but only with full awareness, total detachment, and sacred intent. What would enslave an ordinary man liberates the warrior, because he acts outside a chain of cause and effect having nullified the "doer" within himself.

This practice reshapes the psychic structure. Each detached action becomes a strike against conditioned being, breaking the cycles of compulsion. As Evola states, the true man of Tradition is one who acts "as if he were free," because he is free — not legally or socially, but metaphysically. He has severed the chain at its root: an identification with ego.

Seen through a lens of Radical Tradition, the figure of a Tantric warrior is not utopian. He does not seek to reform society, nor restore lost empires. His concern is not the "world" but Being.

He recognizes that in this age of confusion only the upright path remains. It is a disciplined traversal through the slanting maze of *maya* (illusion), avidly holding to an ascending course.

Tantra provides a living metaphysical framework, while Evola offers a ruthless critique of all that impedes a warrior's path. Together they forge a methodology: live in the world without being of it, act without attachment, master energy through stillness, seek union through polarity, destroy illusion by seeing clearly.

Radical Tradition is not behind, but above. A Tantric Warrior does not look backward; instead, he gazes both inward and upward. In him burns a fire of primordial truth not as memory, but presence. Amid ruins he builds not a stronghold, but bears a flame — his real and sovereign Self.

Magical Idealism and the Power of Consciousness

Ours is a world in which the sacred has been eclipsed by materiality, and man has been reduced to a passive subject of mechanical causality. The doctrine of Magical Idealism offers a radical assertion: consciousness is not a product of this world, but the power over it. In *Essays on Magical Idealism*, Julius Evola articulates a vision of the self not as a conditioned ego, but as a *causa sui* — a self-generating source capable of shaping reality. This is not speculative metaphysics; it is a doctrine of action. It is a call for reestablishing the sovereign subject who actively and concurrently alters both inner and outer worlds through will, awareness, and spiritual discipline.

Such a vision finds echoes in Upanishadic tradition and its Tantric developments. The Tantric path affirms man is not just a receiver of divinity, but also partaker in its insight and even vessel for that same power (śakti) animating the cosmos. From the *mahāvākya* of the *Chāndogya Upanishad* (*"That Thou Art"*) to the astute dictum of the *Bṛhadāraṇyaka* (*"I am Brahman"*), ancient seers intuited what Evola restates in contemporary terms: the Absolute is accessible through self not as concept but as presence — as power.

Evola's philosophical works, particularly *Essays on Magical Idealism*, develop a form of subjectivism in which the world is not an impartial totality, but a field conditioned by quality and orientation of consciousness. Drawing inspiration from Fichte and other post-Kantians, Evola reconfigures their thought in a decisively initiatic and practical direction. For him Self is not an empirical "I" but a supreme, self-positing consciousness (*"I am the I-Am"*) aligned with an Upanishadic conception of *Ātman*.

In this view an act of knowing is now one of being; further, to know oneself as pure awareness exerts a decisive influence on reality. This is the foundational philosophy: our world is not separate from self, but malleable under a force of awakened will. Hence, the task is not escaping this world but assuming control of it, reconfiguring perception and experience around an axis of limitless self — and manifesting it as objective reality.

Tantra, particularly in the *Śākta* and *Kaula* traditions as revealed by Sir John Woodroffe (Arthur Avalon) in *Introduction to Tantra Śāstra* and *The Serpent Power*, affirms perception as divine in essence and mind as its chief instrument of realization. A Tantric adept does not surpass mind through negation, but converts it into a vehicle of liberation through proven methods.

Tantra teaches man's bondage lies in affinity with lower mental patterns (*vṛttis*), and liberation (*mokṣa*) is attained by waking *kuṇḍalinī-śakti*, a latent holy force at the base of one's spine. This is accomplished not via speculation, but *sādhana*: yogic discipline, breath control, visualization, mantra, ritual. These methods seek to activate and refine awareness, making it an intentional actor rather than passive receptacle.

As Woodroffe states, "Man is mind, and through mind he may rise to that which is beyond mind."

This is congruent with Evola's assertion that the spiritual path begins when consciousness no longer reflects the world, but imposes form upon it.

The Tantric way, far from being esoteric theory, is grounded in concrete psycho-physical techniques designed to awaken a dormant power of self. Evola's practical orientation emphasizes that body and breath must be instruments of spiritualization — a view echoed by Eliade, where body is seen not as an obstacle, but a support for transcendence.

Breath (*Prāṇāyāma*)

Breath control regulates and refines the flow of *prāṇa* (vital force). Techniques like *nāḍī-śodhana* (alternate nostril breathing) and *kumbhaka* (breath retention) are means to still the mind, energize the subtle body, and redirect consciousness inward. *Prāṇāyāma* acts upon one's etheric structure, aligning a practitioner with higher states of awareness necessary for inner transformation.

Visualization (*Yantra Nyāsa*)

In visualizing divine symbols (*yantras*) and their placement (*nyāsa*) within a body, one reshapes their inner architecture. The interior world becomes a locus of ritual enactment, replacing passive imagination with will-formed perception. Visualization is a rehearsal of reality in symbolic form — an act of creation, not fantasy.

Recitation (*Mantra Japa*)

Repetition (*japa*) of sacred syllables or formulae (*mantras*) activates vibrational correspondences within. Being subtle form, sound penetrates subconscious, reconfiguring the structure of awareness. In the words of the *Śiva Sūtras*, "The mind itself is mantra." Through mantra an inner sound (*nāda*) is a medium for raising consciousness.

These practices are not simply ends in themselves. They are instruments for generating a new ontological state. It is one in which an individual becomes a center of power rather than prey to circumstances seemingly beyond their control.

The origin of Vedāntic and Tantric metaphysics known as the *Upanishads* articulate a primacy of consciousness in explicit terms.

In the *Kaṭha Upanishad*, Yama states:

एको वशी सर्वभूतान्तरात्मा एकं रूपं बहुधा यः करोति

Eko vaśī sarvabhūtāntarātmā ekam
rūpaṁ bahudhā yaḥ karoti

"The one controller, the Self within all beings,
makes the one form into many."
(*Kaṭha Upanishad* II.2.12)

This insight corresponds exactly to Evola's Magical Idealism. A multiplicity of experience is based in a singular, independent Self that shapes the world from within. It is One inside and out.

Similarly, the *Muṇḍaka Upanishad* declares:

ब्रह्मैवेदममृतं पुरस्ताद्ब्रह्म पश्चाद्ब्रह्म दक्षिणतश्चोत्तरेण

Brahmaivedam amṛtaṁ purastād brahma
paścād brahma dakṣiṇataścottareṇa

"Brahman is all this —
before, behind, to the right and the left."
(*Muṇḍaka* II.2.11)

Such verses affirm there is no "outside" of consciousness; all phenomena arise within it and all change begins through it. Armed with these insights, a Tantric practitioner works to align his microcosmic center (*ātman*) with a comprehensive reality (*brahman*) via controlled practice, not passive contemplation.

Our contemporary world is one of fragmentation, nihilism, and distraction — a theme repeatedly emphasized in *Ride the Tiger*. Evola's analysis of modernity explains how an individual is assaulted by horizontal forces: consumerism, relativism, technological saturation, and psychological dispersion. These separate man from a vertical dimension, and hence his link to transcendent reality.

Against this backdrop, consciousness becomes a battlefield and its mastery the precondition for resistance. Evola calls for an inner stance of detachment and control — not in the stoic or moralistic sense, but a Tantric one. This is a means to engage this world without being soiled by it, using experience as fuel for transcendence while empowering the highest self.

This idea is also at the heart of the *Bhagavad Gītā*, where Krishna tells Arjuna:

योगस्थ: कुरु कर्माणि सङ्गं त्यक्त्वा धनञ्जय

Yogasthaḥ kuru karmāṇi saṅgaṁ tyaktvā dhanañjaya

"Perform action, O Arjuna,
established in yoga, abandoning attachment."
(*Gītā* II.48)

This is not resignation, but sovereign action — karma rooted in awareness. It is the ideal of a detached warrior: one who acts with precision not because he desires an outcome, but because it is his nature to act with excellence (*svadharma*). In this way, Magical Idealist and Tantric Yogi converge in that both act in the world without becoming bound to it.

The goal then is not escapism or mysticism in a conventional sense, but integration of all faculties (body, breath, speech, and mind) into a singular direction of will. Evola speaks of the "transcendental self" as one emerging through concentration, interiorization, and disciplined action. This is not an abstract ideal, but a real and attainable potentiality.

A spiritual warrior must anchor his mind through breath and mantra, breaking free of psychic conditioning. It is also essential he refine perception through visualization and ritual, turning daily life into symbolic action. He should likewise maintain physical strength and stillness, understanding the body is not corrupt but sacred when governed by spirit.

Finally, he acts decisively without attachment, recognizing every moment as a trial of inner sovereignty. In the final analysis, Magical Idealism and Tantra converge in their vision of man as a creative, formative force. Both approaches affirm reality takes shape according to the quality of one's awareness, and that the path to liberation lies not in rejection, but active mastery.

In Upanishadic terms Self (*Ātman*) is not an object. It is pure witnessing presence — conscious, free, and luminous.

ज्योतिषामपि तज्ज्योतिस्तमसः परमुच्यते

Jyotīṣām api taj jyotiḥ tamasaḥ param ucyate

"That is the Light of all lights, beyond all darkness."
(*Gītā* XIII.17)

The aim of *sadhana* is personifying this truth; the task of a Tantric warrior is living it moment by moment. Consciousness rightly understood and directed is the sword, flame, and axis upon which a fallen world may be redeemed — not outwardly, but an inner revolt. The battlefield is within and victory belongs to those who see with clarity, act with detachment, and burn with unwavering will.

Ritual in Tantric Practice

Ritual functions as the metaphysical scaffolding of spiritual experience. True and effective ritual is rooted in cosmic order (*Ṛta*); it bridges the absolute and manifest, carrying symbolic principles through time-bound form. Symbols are expressions of a supra-human principle. When ritual fades, mankind slips into chaos, formlessness, and pseudo-religion.

Evola echoes this necessity, describing ritual as an external expression of vertical intent. It serves as a controlled theatre where one aligns to a cosmic underpinning, ensuring experience remains anchored to a metaphysical hierarchy.

When experienced, ritual becomes a vertical moment in an otherwise horizontal world. It trains the practitioner to carry sacred presence into mundane encounters, act without losing center, and anchor freedom in form. Ritual is "order through structure," turning consciousness into a transmitting node of tradition rather than pustule of modern sentiment.

Ritual habits are not escapism, but actualization forming reserves of life force and linking sacred presence. Faced with modern chaos — information overload, distraction, purposeless drift — ritual creates and reinforces a meta-space. It brings one into unity with cosmic order, aligning inner and outer realms.

For both Guénon and Evola, ritual is not a relic but a tool of legitimacy, weapon of structure, and most importantly vector of continuity. When performed regularly, properly, and sincerely, even a modest ritual becomes a pillar of self-governance and an alliance with Traditional forces. It is how power activates form, intention evokes energy, and one conducts a symphony of Spirit.

Ritual acts as a metaphysical support of spiritual experience. It is intrinsic to Tradition, not a peripheral embellishment. René Guénon writes that ritual is "a support in traditional law, with its objective and supra-personal character, and is symbolically expressed by traditional states or empires."

It is a structural character as ritual maintaining the bridge between absolute and manifest, grounding spiritual existence in temporality. Symbols therein represent a "non-human principle" serving as ontological languages that cannot be replaced by modern psychological or metaphorical substitutes. Absent holy ritual we drift into ephemera, pseudo-religiosity, disorder, and vapid sentimentality.

Evola emphasizes the necessity of ritual as a disciplined theatre in which human will aligns with cosmic hierarchy. When properly accomplished, ritual becomes a vertical moment — a center of gravity forming a focal point in life. Through ritual the practitioner cultivates a sacred presence, carrying it into the world without losing their equipoise. In today's era of sensory overload and constant distraction, ritual is essential to resisting a purposeless, perpetual drift of vague sentience.

Traditional societies relied on hierarchies "suspended" from a metaphysical center; when hierarchy disappears, societies devolve into a mass of disorder. Ritual customs then become much like using a rudder to right a ship set adrift. This metaspace provides firm clarity amid anarchic sophistication and aligns inner psychic order with an outer cosmic harmony.

Guénon and Evola agree that Traditionally-inspired ritual is a repository of sacred validity, deterrent against involution, and bond between related eras and peoples.

"Tradition, in its essence, is something simultaneously meta-historical and dynamic: it is an overall ordering force in the service of principles that have the chrism of a superior legitimacy."—Evola

Each ritual act is a direct link to transcendent principles. The priest tending an eternal fire "saved the city through his ritual, day after day." Equally, a failure in ritual obligations is not just negligence, but metaphysical breach: "[a rite that fails] wounds and defaces a 'god': it is *sacrilegium.*"

When ritual is performed regularly, correctly, and sincerely, even its simplest form becomes a pillar of spiritual imperium. It promotes lineage, authority, and cosmic resonance. Likewise, one is cultivating an alliance with Traditional forces.

Each enactment becomes a feat of power activating form and intention evoking energy. The present-day ritualist conducts a symphony of Spirit in an otherwise profane, dissonant world.

Ritual is a gateway through which ontological perception becomes lived reality. Deprived of it we dwell in chaos and nihilism. With it we educe a sacred elan, becoming beacons of Tradition and building inner fortitude against modern decay.

A sincere, authentic ritual life is not escapism, performance art, or nostalgia; it is strategic, sovereign, and holy. By practicing and preserving true ritual one participates in an eternal flow, ensuring Tradition exists through intention, act, and presence.

"The essential task ahead requires formulating an adequate doctrine… an elite differentiating itself… will be the bearer of a new principle of higher authority and sovereignty." —Evola

The Polarities of Shiva and Shakti

A worldview rooted in metaphysical hierarchy and opposed to material egalitarianism assumes the cosmos is not a random collection of phenomena, but an ordered field controlled by primordial opposites. Essential to all of these is the polarity of Shiva and Shakti — not as mythological figures, but archetypal binaries: consciousness and energy, force and form, immobility and dynamism, transcendence and immanence. In the context of Radical Tradition this sacred duality is not to be worshipped but understood, assumed, and applied.

Where mainstream neo-Tantra often collapses into feminine-centered emotionalism and erotic permissiveness, Evola affirms a stern, masculine, vertical accent on Tantric practice. Drawing on Nietzschean thought via an Evolian lens, we locate within the Shiva-Shakti dynamic a theoretical and practical framework for integrating and transcending opposites.

This is not through fusion, but dominance of higher over lower, form over flux, being over becoming. In philosophic terms this is a will-to-power, though not principally expressed in dominion over others. It is instead mastery of self, chiefly by taming or repurposing chaotic and degraded forces.

In classical Tantric metaphysics as elucidated by Woodroffe (Avalon), Shiva is *cit*: pure, undifferentiated consciousness. He is *akriyā* — the non-acting principle of absolute stillness. Shakti by contrast is dynamic force, movement, manifestation (*śakti*). Hers is a becoming that dances upon the formless substratum of Shiva. She is *kriyā-śakti* — an active, creative energy without which nothing arises.

Their union is ontological. The Śiva-Śakti dynamic is a fusion of opposites: a play of the formless using form to express itself. Shakti has no meaning without Shiva; Shiva is inert without Shakti. But — and this is essential in the Evolian interpretation — it is Shiva who provides the axis: *he* is an unmoved mover around which all spirals.

In Tantric visualization the two are signified through *liṅga* (phallus) and *yoni* (womb), or in energetic terms as feminine *kuṇḍalinī-śakti* ascending toward *sahasrāra*: the crown where masculine Śiva consciousness is fully awakened. The polarity is thus both cosmic and intimate, reflected in general dynamics and individual realization.

Evola repeatedly warns against the modern degeneration of spiritual paths into sentimentality, sensualism, and passivity. He identifies in *Ride the Tiger* a trend toward gynocracy in both religion and culture: a dissolution of form-giving, Apollonian masculinity in favor of chaos, passion, and atavism. While often understood as exalting a feminine principle, in Evola's reading — consistent with authentic Shaivite doctrines — Tantra sees a primacy of the masculine pole as necessary for liberation.

Whereas *Śākta* traditions elevate the feminine to a sovereign status — sometimes to a point of reversing metaphysical order — the Shaivite-Tantric path outlined in *Yoga of Power* insists upon hierarchy and transcendence. The sacred masculine is not reactive, but axial; it does not dissolve into Shakti, but stands immovable, drawing her upward, sublimating her. This is the Solar path in contrast to Lunar cults, which may unleash forces not able to be subdued or rerouted by an initiate.

Thus, a true union of Shiva and Shakti is not eroticism or devotional ecstasy, but ritual polarity wherein a practitioner embodying Shiva enters into relation with energy (Shakti) to master, transmute, and rise above it. The *Vīra*, or heroic adept, approaches Shakti not to be overwhelmed, but to integrate her force into his solar axis.

The archetype of *Kālī*, especially in her darker aspects, epitomizes untamed feminine energy — death, desire, time, and transformation. In the context of modernity this archetype has become unconsciously embodied in the disorderly, destabilizing sexual and emotional forces that dominate our post-traditional West: a rise of anti-hierarchical values, the collapse of sentience into sensation, and a subversion of natural roles in bad faith.

Evola's critique of modern sexual relations in *Ride the Tiger*, especially in the chapter "Relations Between the Sexes," exposes how a "liberated" feminine principle unmoored from Tradition begets not utopia but chaos. Conversely, a Tantric adept does not seek to repress these forces, nor moralize as subtle control. Instead he entices, accesses, and directs this energy.

Here the comparison is alchemical. As a dissolutive force of time and change *Kālī* — the destructive feminine aspect — is raw power (*śakti*). The masculine task is not to worship her blindly, but assume the role of *Mahākāla* — Shiva in his terrible, still aspect as time beyond time — and thus tame her through higher being. This does not imply control in a psychological sense, but mastery in a metaphysical one.

In Evola's view there is an affinity between will, vital energy, and spiritual substance conceptualized in Tantric and esoteric language as *prāṇa*, *ojas*, and more recently "*Vril*." This life-force is not to be wasted, but cultivated and directed through ritual discipline, bodily integrity, and positive asceticism.

Tantra, especially in its heroic (*Vīra*) form, presents concrete techniques for harnessing this energy. *Prāṇāyāma*, or breath control, not only oxygenates but concentrates and directs subtle energy, enhancing will and stilling the mind. *Bandhas* (muscular locks) and *mudrās* stabilize a flow of energy within the *suṣumnā nāḍī*, allowing an ascent of *kuṇḍalinī-śakti*. *Brahmacarya* (control of sexual energy) and *mantra-japa* generate heat (*tapas*) that transforms raw vitality into holy power.

All this posits a warrior ethic: no indulgence, romanticism, or diffusion of force. This is an alchemical transformation of lead into gold. From a Tantric standpoint sex must serve transformation, not gratification. A ritual union (*maithuna*) when properly approached is not erotic but initiatic. It is a ritual of polarity meant to combine Shakti as force with Shiva as awareness, with the latter retaining autonomous detachment throughout.

In Evolian metaphysics the task is not synthesis, but ascent: to move from variety to unity, becoming to being, as a means to surpass illusion. Rightly understood the Shiva-Shakti polarity is not a license for indulgence, but template for inner conquest. Shaivism does not elevate the feminine; it sublimates her fire to fuel masculine transcendence. The virile adept does not reject the world, but reshapes it — just as Shakti, when mastered, becomes a vehicle for Shiva's awakening.

This is the true path of a Tantric warrior in the Kali Yuga: not to blend into the chaos of egalitarian worship and formless spiritualism, but to stand like Shiva — aloof, terrible, immovable — while harnessing Shakti as means, as sacrament. In this, we achieve an ideal of the Solar path as a magical hero. He is one who knows the world begins where a self wills it.

As the *Śvetāśvatara Upanishad* declares:

तं एव विदित्वाती मृत्युंति नान्यः पन्था विद्यतेऽयनायाः

Tameva viditvāti mṛtyumeti nānyaḥ panthā vidyate ayanāya

"Only by knowing Him (the Self) does one pass beyond death; there is no other path."

So too does the Tantric warrior, grounded in Shiva, master Shakti — and through this polarity, surpass all opposition.

Mantra and the Science of Sound

The science of mantra lies at the heart of Tantra as a precise metaphysical technology. Mantra operates as a vibrational key to unlock latent energies of awareness, bridging the visible and invisible, the individual and transcendent. Evola's *Yoga of Power* highlights mantra as a tool of inner transformation, aligned with a Tantric warrior's aim to dominate subtle forces within himself and project influence onto the world through awakened will.

Mantra is a formulaic sound-seed (*bīja*) that carries both psychic and cosmic potency. According to John Woodroffe (Arthur Avalon) in his *Introduction to Tantra Śāstra*, a mantra is "the sound-body of a deity." It is a living vibration which, when properly activated, manifests a divine force within. The mantra is not a symbol of divinity; it is divinity in sonic form.

The *Kṣurikā Upaniṣad* says:

मननात् त्रायते इति मन्त्रः

Mananāt trāyate iti mantraḥ

"That which protects (trāyate) through contemplation (manana) is mantra."

This etymological definition captures the double-action of mantra: it both focuses the mind and protects consciousness from descent into fragmentation or entropy. It is a precise technology intended for those who do not pray to gods, but become them.

Tantric metaphysics affirms sound (*śabda*) precedes form (*rūpa*), a belief aligned with the Vedic doctrine of *Vāk* (speech). In its fourfold structure — *Parā*, *Paśyantī*, *Madhyamā*, and *Vaikharī* — this maps a descent of sound from unmanifest into expression. The *Rigveda* declares:

अ॒हमे॒व स्व॒यमि॒दं व॑दामि॒ जुष्टं॑ दे॒वेभि॑रु॒त मानु॑षेभिः

Aham eva svayam idam vadāmi
juṣṭaṃ devebhir uta mānuṣebhiḥ

"I myself speak this that is dear to gods and men."

Sound is not an empirical phenomenon, but logoic resonance materialized as vibration. In other words, sound precedes and undergirds all reality. In *Yoga of Power*, Evola affirms this when he states that true initiation involves "aligning oneself with the cosmic rhythm" of which mantra is a sonic manifestation.

Consciousness is not passive — it shapes reality. Mantra is one of the tools through which an awakened will directs energy. Evola viewed a Tantric use of sound as a method of domination over internal and external worlds. The sacred syllables function as carriers of psychic and spiritual vibration. Recited with full awareness and intent, they become invocations of forces that reconfigure not only an individual psyche but the very energetic matrix of the cosmos.

Mantra is not external to mind — it is the mind in its purest, vibratory state. From an Evolian perspective this indicates a profound link between engagement and efficacy. An adept does not "repeat" mantras mechanically, but partakes in a vibrational consonance with them.

Each mantra has specific resonance with the subtle centers (*cakras*) — psycho-cosmological loci through which *kundalinī* rises. This internal architecture is crucial to understanding the functional aspect of sound in Tantric practice. Specific *bīja mantras* (seed syllables) correspond to elemental energies and the cakras: *Lam* (Earth), *Mūlādhāra* (Root); *Vam* (Water), *Svādhiṣṭhāna* (Sacral); *Ram* (Fire), *Maṇipūra* (Solar Plexus); *Yam* (Air), *Anāhata* (Heart); *Ham* (Ether), *Viśuddha* (Throat); *Om* (Mind), *Ājñā* (Third Eye). Likewise, *Hroum* is an esoteric *bīja* associated with transcendental Shiva power and often linked to *sahasrāra* via secret transmissions in kula and krama systems.

By chanting these mantras with concentrated intent, the practitioner awakens and harmonizes these centers. The ascent of *kundalinī* is aided by vibrational resonance. The sound both summons and stabilizes the energy at each station of being.

Tantric texts consistently affirm the vibrational structure of the universe. This also implies that by following the vibration of a mantra inward — beyond the gross utterance — one reaches a stillness of pure consciousness (*śiva-tattva*). It is not the sound alone, but an intent and awareness accompanying it that determines its transformative power.

A practical *sādhana* involving mantra proceeds as follows:

1. Setting the Intention (*Saṅkalpa*): A practitioner sits with back straight, legs crossed in *siddhāsana* or other seated yogic pose (explained in a future chapter). He mentally affirms his *saṅkalpa* (intention) to awaken sovereignty through vibration.

2. Centering with *Prāṇāyāma:* Breathe deeply through the nose and from the abdomen. Perform three rounds of alternate nostril breathing (*nāḍī-śodhana*) to balance psychic energies.

3. Mantra Japa (*Om* and *Hroum*): With a (*rudrākṣa) mālā* of 108 beads, begin *mantra japa. "Om"* is intoned for 54 beads. The sound should rise from the navel and culminate at the third eye. This mantra is the *pranava*: a cosmic hum of creation and dissolution. *"Hroum"* is then chanted for the remaining 54 beads. This sound encapsulates a fierce, radiant power of *Śiva* in his transformative aspect. It cuts through illusion (*avidyā*) and penetrates into the subtle field of being. Each mantra is to be heard internally, not just uttered. The vibration must be felt in the body — especially through the chest, spine, and skull.

4. Visualization and Ascent: Visualize a light ascending the spine with each utterance. Awakened by the mantra's sound, see each cakra spinning with light. When finished, sit in silence to let the subtle field settle. Remain alert and lucid — no opinions or analysis should ensue.

5. Closure: Bow the head and make an *anjali mudrā* (prayer gesture), chanting *"Śivoham" ("I am Śiva")* three times. Seal the energy by pressing one's tongue to the palate (*kechari mudrā*).

Evola draws implicit connections between Tantric sound science and the Western concept of Logos. Just as mantras are not merely phonetic but vibrational entities that form reality, so too Logos is a principle of divine reason articulated as creative word in esotericism. Traditionalist metaphysics asserts all true spiritual systems recognize that sound is power, and spoken vibration when ritually enacted is *actio sacra* ("sacred action").

To chant a mantra in the Tantric sense is not to ask or plead. It is to command, invoke, and ultimately become. The Evolian adept does not chant to escape the world, nor to dissolve into formlessness. He recites to dominate the inner forces, to master illusion, and to ascend.

The science of sound is thus a royal path for the virile and awake. It views the cosmos as a vibratory structure, and self as both its instrument and wielder.

Yantra:
Geometry of the Divine

Yantras ("instruments") occupy a central place in Tantra, embodying cosmic principles through geometrical diagrams. These unfold against a backdrop of traditional metaphysics. *Yantras* serve not merely as devotional images but implements of inner order, structuring one's subtle realms and projecting intent into the manifested world.

Arthur Avalon affirms *yantras* are "plastic objects" serving as three-dimensional maps of divine forces. Among them, the *Śrī Yantra* (or *Sri Chakra*) is paramount. It is composed of nine interpenetrating triangles — four pointing up (symbolizing *Śiva*) and five down (signifying *Śakti*) — forming forty-three sub-triangles arranged concentrically around a *bindu*, the ultimate point of unity. It is both an image of cosmos and "microcosmic body" enabling one to externalize their spiritual evolution.

The *Śrī Yantra* is sometimes called *yantra-rāja* ("king of yantras"). Its pattern reflects nine *āvaranas* (enclosures) — from the four-gated square (*bhupara*) to the *bindu* at the center — symbolizing stages of cosmos and levels of consciousness.

Upward (*Śiva*) triangles represent limitation, consciousness, and transcendent will. Downward (*Śakti*) triangles represent manifestation, energy, and immanent force. Their joining signifies an interplay of cosmological principles mapping to stages of emanation and absorption.

The *bindu* is *Citiśakti*, the point where all duality collapses; it is silence, unity, the transcendent Self. The surrounding lotus petals symbolize *āṇḍa* (cosmic eggs) and developmental levels of consciousness. The external square is the *Bhūpura*, protecting the sacred interior.

The *Bhāvana Upaniṣad* (a *Śākta Upanishad*) explicitly equates the human body to a *Śrī Chakra*, teaching that internal worship of its geometry awakens *Ātmā* as *Śakti*. The *Tripurātāpinī Upaniṣad* likewise states union of *Śiva* and *Śakti* is the source of all being and *yantra* and *chakra* are paths to that revelation.

Simpler and more particularized to this Rite, a *Śiva yantra* maps masculine consciousness. This is comprised of an upward-pointing triangle, *bindu*, and frame (see introductory graphic).

Yantra creation is Magical Idealism in practice: mind projects form as an inner structure, and form shapes outward reality the way tensioned geometry structures energy. Through *nyāsa* a practitioner "takes possession" of the yantra's energy. It consequently becomes both an inner organon and external field of influence, harmonizing microcosm with macrocosm and manifesting will in the world. Accordingly, *yantras* are visual entry points into levels of consciousness and frequencies of energetic resonance.

Śiva Yantra Construction

Draw an upward equilateral triangle with a central *bindu* on a piece of metal, paper, or wood. Surround it with a square frame. Consecrate it through the following ritual.

Placing a candle or oil lamp (*Diya*) at each corner, purify it by sprinkling water and lighting incense (*Dhupa*). Perform *bīja-nyāsa* vocalizing "*Hroum*" three times, mentally placing the sound into the *bindu*. Chant "*Oṁ Namaḥ Śivāya*" 108 times while gazing softly at the yantra. Visualize the triangle expanding light into your pineal center. Seal by reciting "*Svaha.*"

Use this *yantra* daily. Sit before it, breathe quietly, repeating *"Śivoham."* A triangular shape acts as an anchor for structured consciousness formation. Daily contemplations should involve gazing and gradually shifting attention from edges to *bindu.*

This practice itself begins with *Nyāsa* of *Hroum* and focused gazing (*dhyāna*) at the *bindu* — sense binding between internal and external geometry. Transition to a silent repetition of the *mantra* while holding the yantra in the mind's eye. Then begin mentally tracing the *yantra's* lines inward to its *bindu*, unifying breath, gaze, and awareness. Close reciting *"Śivoham" ("I am Śiva")*; bow the head and make an *anjali mudrā* (prayer gesture).

The *tantrika* aligned with Radical Tradition uses yantra not to fantasize or seek wholeness by dissolving form. He masters form through will, engaging with a transcendent center through intentional alignment. He restyles his inner and outer territories into domains of sacrality, order, and power.

The yantra is both mirror and tool — it reflects cosmos and reframes a practitioner. In its concentric, interlocking geometry, inner and outer coincide. In the center, beyond duality, is the silence of supreme being. A yantra becomes an architectural enactment of the phrase "became what you beheld." Thought becomes form, and form invokes awareness.

Yantras are geometric manifestations of metaphysical being, instruments for transforming one's self and surroundings. Through them, a Tantric warrior constructs strongholds of sacred order and projects that outward. From a standpoint of Magical Idealism, a yantra is an intentional inscription of consciousness upon reality — an impression of will upon form. When approached with reverence, fervor, and attention, *yantra* is an expression of sacred geometry and route to sovereignty, command, and congruence.

Constructing *yantras* demands precision and awareness. A symbol is inert without conscious vitality behind it. Conversely, when built with intention (*saṅkalpa*), mathematical exactness, and ritual protocol (sanctification, mantra, and visualization) it becomes a sacred engine, organizing both psyche and setting in harmony with cosmic order.

Body as Sacred Vessel

Far more than a biological shell, the body is a microcosm of the cosmos imbued with a latent potential for transcendence. From an Evolian perspective it represents a battlefield: a site for mastering primal energies, forging inner sovereignty, and attaining vertical liberation. In this vein, Hatha Yoga practices prepare the body as a sacred vessel for transformation.

The subtle body features an intricate network of *nāḍīs* — energy channels that carry *prāṇa*, the vital force. Indic tradition names three primary *nāḍīs*: *sūṣumṇā* at the spine's center, *iḍā* on the left, and *piṅgalā* on the right. *Iḍā* and *piṅgalā* cross one another at chakra junctions and merge at the *ajñā* chakra (the "third eye"). The *sūṣumṇā* serves as a spiritual corridor through which energies align and transcendence unfolds.

Iḍā — associated with lunar, intuitive energy — is cooling and nurturing while *piṅgalā* — linked to solar action — is dynamic and warming. When one nostril flows more easily (or the other is blocked) it typically indicates which *nāḍī* dominates. Balancing flow through *iḍā* and *piṅgalā* stabilizes the mental-emotional field and prepares a central channel for spiritual ascent. Hatha Yoga is energetic hygiene purifying this subtle network through a tri-fold regimen: *āṣana* (postures), *bandha* (energetic locks), and *prāṇāyāma* (breath control).

Foundational Āsanas for Tantric Discipline

Proper seated posture (*āsana*) forms a vital foundation for Tantric practice. Classic positions like *siddhāsana*, *padmāsana*, and *bhuadhrāsana* ground the spine and pelvis enabling stable energetic alignment. These are not mere physical exercises but sacred geometries aligning gross and subtle bodies. They prepare one's body to become a throne of awareness. When assumed correctly they stabilize *prāṇa*, focus mind, and foster tranquility.

1. *Siddhāsana* (सिद्धासन) — "The Accomplished Pose"

Siddhāsana is lauded in Tantric and yogic texts as the preeminent meditative seat. According to the *Hatha Yoga Pradīpikā*, it is considered the best *āsana* for spiritual realization, because it helps stabilize the body and control the nervous system.

सिद्धासनं प्रपन्नो यस्तु योगी न सिध्यति।

किमन्यैर्बहुभिर्दोषैः सिद्धासनं समाचरेत्॥

Siddhāsanaṁ prapanno yastu yogī na sidhyati
Kimanyairbahubhirdoṣaiḥ siddhāsanaṁ samācaret

"He who sits in siddhāsana and controls the breath cannot fail to attain siddhi. What use are other āsanas?"

How to Perform Siddhāsana: Sit on the floor with legs extended forward. Bend the left leg and bring the heel to press firmly against the perineum. Bend the right leg and place the right ankle over the left ankle, so that the heel is just above the genitals (pressing lightly on the pubic bone). The toes of both feet should be tucked between the opposite calf and thigh, hidden from view. Keep the spine erect and the head balanced directly above the torso. Rest the hands on the knees in *chin mudrā* (palms up, thumbs and forefingers touching, and others extended). Close the eyes and bring the awareness inward.

Benefits and role in Tantric practice: This *āsana* creates energetic pressure on the *mūlādhāra* and stabilizes the pelvis, making it ideal for *mūla* bandha and *prāṇāyāma*. It stimulates the upward flow of *kundalinī* and balances the *iḍā* and *piṅgalā nāḍīs*. It also minimizes movement, supporting long periods of meditation and *mantra japa*.

2. *Padmāsana* (पद्मासन) — "The Lotus Pose"

Padmāsana is the classical lotus posture symbolizing purity and divine detachment. Frequently associated with both *Śiva* and the Buddha, this *āsana* offers supreme stability for energy alignment and meditative trance (*dhyāna*). The *Gheraṇḍa Saṁhitā* describes it as the seat of yogic mastery:

पद्मं सुसंस्थाय विधाय हस्तौ दृष्टिं नासाग्रे विनियोजयित्वा।

सम्यग्गतेनाधरपृष्ठबद्धं ध्यानं करोत्यात्मविमुक्तिहेतुम्॥

Padmaṁ susaṁsthāya vidhāya hastau dṛṣṭiṁ nāsāgre viniyojayitvā samyaggatenādharapṛṣṭhabaddhaṁ dhyānaṁ karotyātmavimuktihetum

"Seated in padmāsana, with hands in mudrā, gaze fixed at the nose-tip, the yogī may meditate to attain self-liberation."

How to perform Padmāsana: Sit with legs extended. Place the right foot on the left thigh so that the sole faces upward and heel is near the navel. Bring the left foot on top of the right thigh in the same manner. Ensure both knees rest comfortably on the ground and spine is perfectly upright. Hands may rest on the knees in *chin mudrā*. Breath should be even and awareness directed to the third eye or the heart center.

Cautions: This *āsana* requires flexibility in the hips and knees, and it should be approached gently and incrementally. Practitioners should begin with *ardha-padmasana* (half-lotus), whereas those with joint issues may remain in *siddhāsana*.

Tantric Utility: *Padmāsana* establishes a symmetrical foundation for breath retention, subtle energy circulation, and mantra recitation. It forms the geometric base of the subtle body's vertical axis and is ideal for *kuṇḍalinī* work and visualization exercises.

3. *Bhadrāsana* (भद्रासन) — "The Auspicious or Gracious Pose"

Bhadrāsana is also known as *baddha-koṇāsana* in present-day yogic parlance. It is valued in Tantric ritual for its grounding qualities and role in activating the pelvic region and lower *nāḍīs*. It is often a preliminary pose for more advanced seated ones.

How to perform Bhadrāsana: Sit with the spine erect and legs extended. Bend the knees and bring the soles of the feet together. Draw the heels inward toward the perineum as closely as possible.

Grasp the feet or ankles with both hands. Gently press the knees downward with the elbows or let them fall naturally. Keep the spine straight and shoulders relaxed. Close the eyes and breathe deeply, allowing the hips to open.

Modifications: If knees remain high, sit on a folded blanket or block to lift the pelvis, facilitating external hip rotation.

Tantric Value: This posture is excellent for accessing *apānic* (downward-moving) *prāṇa*. It balances reproductive energies and prepares a pelvic floor for *mūla bandha* and other subtle locks. It is also stabilizing for use in longer rituals or extended *mantra japa* sessions.

Each posture stabilizes an energetic system, supporting the spine for meditative alignment and creating a physical geometry required for internal stillness and activation. The warrior-yogi is anchored in bodily command, not intangible detachment. These *āsanas* give form to that ideal: a body held in stillness, breath in control, will in mastery — becoming the temple of *Śiva* wherein *Śakti* rises.

Bandhas: Locks of Power and Ascent

Bandhas — *mūla bandha* (pelvic lift), *uḍḍiyāna bandha* (abdominal lock), and *jālandhāra bandha* (chin lock) — contain and direct *prāṇa*, preparing deeper energetic activation. These physical preparations condition a subtle body to support higher practices without disruptive leakage or side effects. In the framework of Tantric discipline, bandhas (energetic locks) are instruments of interior authority.

Each lock functions to redirect, contain, and elevate the flow of *prāṇa* within a subtle body, especially in preparation for *kuṇḍalinī-śakti* to climb the *suṣumṇā-nāḍī*. According to Avalon's *The Serpent Power*, these bandhas act as yantric seals within a bodily temple, allowing an aspirant to break from the dissipative tendencies of ordinary desire and rechannel bio-spiritual energy upward toward union with the Absolute (*Paramātman*).

1. *Mūla* Bandha (मूलबन्ध) — "Root Lock"

Mūla bandha is considered foundational, activating the *mūlādhāra* chakra, the seat of dormant *kuṇḍalinī*. The *Hatha Yoga Pradīpikā* describes it thus:

मूलबन्धं समासीनो यो बिभर्ति दिनं क्षणं।

युवावपि जरामृत्युं तस्य नास्ति कथंचन॥

Mūlabandhaṁ samāsīno yo bibharti dinaṁ kṣaṇaṁ
Yuvāv api jarāmṛtyuṁ tasya nāsti kathaṁcana

"He who holds the root lock for even a moment each day, even if young, escapes old age and death."

How to perform Mūla Bandha: Sit in a meditative posture (*siddhāsana* or *padmāsana).* Focus awareness on the perineum (area between the anus and the genitals). Contract the pelvic floor muscles, drawing the perineum upward. The contraction should be subtle and internal, not involving the thighs or buttocks. Incorporate breath retention upon inhaling (*antara kumbhaka*) while holding this lock.

Spiritual and Energetic Effects: *Mūla* bandha awakens the root chakra, seals downward-dissipating energy, and begins an ascent of *apāna* into *prāṇa*, allowing for their union. This action is one of willful inner conquest — seizing animal erotic drives and turning them into fuel for transcendence. It also supports a practice of *brahmacarya* (energetic continence) as a basis of all higher Tantric operations.

2. *Uḍḍiyāna* Bandha (उड्डीयान बन्ध) — "Upward-Flying Lock"

This lock is associated with the abdominal region and is considered the most powerful of the three primary bandhas. *The Gheraṇḍa Saṁhitā* states:

उड्डीयानं तु नाम बन्धं कठिनं कृतं प्रयत्नतः।

अभ्यासेन तु यो विद्वान् स शिवत्वाय कल्पते॥

Uḍḍīyānaṁ tu nāma bandhaṁ kaṭhinaṁ kṛtaṁ prayatnataḥ
Abhyāsena tu yo vidvān sa śivatvāya kalpate

"That which flies upward is uḍḍiyāna bandha; though difficult, it leads to Śiva-consciousness when mastered."

How to perform Uḍḍiyāna Bandha: Stand with feet shoulder-width apart. Bend the knees slightly and place hands on the thighs. Exhale completely through the nose. After exhalation, without inhaling, perform a mock inhalation by expanding the ribcage and lifting the chest, while keeping the glottis closed. This action draws the abdominal organs inward and upward, forming a concave hollow below the ribcage. Hold the lock for several seconds (or as long as comfortable), then gently release and inhale.

Note: This bandha should be learned only after mastering breath awareness and exhalation control. It is not to be done after meals or by those with hypertension.

Spiritual and Energetic Effects: *Uḍḍiyāna bandha* activates the solar plexus and draws lower energies up toward the heart center. It harmonizes *samāna* and *udāna prāṇas*, facilitating mental clarity, *prāṇic* control, and eventual access to the higher chakras. Evola would frame this as the warrior's upward impulse — the "flight toward the sun," a conscious inversion of the downward gravitational pull of matter and entropy. In Tantric *sādhanā*, this lock ensures inner fire (*agni*) and serpent energy are directed not toward dissolution, but sublimation.

3. *Jālandhāra Bandha* (जालन्धर बन्ध) — "Throat Lock"

Jālandhāra bandha regulates the flow of energy to the brain and controls the *bindu* (sacred fluid), preventing its dissipation. *The Hatha Yoga Pradīpikā* declares:

जालन्धरस्य बन्धस्य निधनेन हठादिना।

बद्धे कण्ठे पदं याति सन्मार्गेण सहस्वना॥

Jālandharasya bandhasya nidhanena haṭhādinā
Baddhe kaṇṭhe padaṁ yāti sanmārgeṇa sahasvanā

"With the throat lock held by forceful yoga, the path of the nectar and breath is stabilized and directed upward."

How to Perform Jālandhāra Bandha: Sit in a comfortable meditative posture with spine straight. Inhale deeply, hold the breath (*antar kumbhaka*), and tuck the chin into the notch of the sternum. Simultaneously lift the chest slightly to lengthen the cervical spine. Engage the throat muscles gently without strain, sealing off the upward flow. Release the lock slowly before exhalation.

Cautions: Always perform this bandha with an empty stomach and only after mastering breath retention. Avoid in cases of high blood pressure or cervical spine issues.

Spiritual and Energetic Effects: This lock restricts and guides the flow of *amṛta* (nectar of immortality) that drips from the *bindu visarga*, preventing its dissipation into the digestive fire (*jatharagni*). It also blocks erratic mental chatter and supports entry into meditative stillness. In Evolian terms, it symbolizes a containment of thought and strategic redirection of awareness upward toward the metaphysical center. In conjunction with *kumbhaka*, it completes the energetic seal needed for deep Tantric visualization and mantra-based awakening.

When performed together — especially in seated practice after *prāṇāyāma* — these three bandhas function as energetic seals that close the lower gates and redirect life-force energy toward the spinal axis and subtle centers. *Mūla bandha* stops downward flow at the root, *uḍḍiyāna* draws energy upward through the navel, and *jālandhāra* seals the head, focusing internal pressure at the third eye.

Together, they form the *Yogic Seal of Sovereignty*, ensuring that the body — now stabilized, aligned, and internalized — becomes a sacred vessel for Tantric action, visualization, and ascent. For an Evolian adept, mastery of the bandhas is akin to building a sacred citadel within which an inner fire may blaze and from which a holy war can be waged.

Breath as Blade and Flame

Prāṇāyāma occupies a vital role in opening and harmonizing *nāḍīs*. Practices like *nāḍī-śodhana* (alternate nostril breathing) methodically balance *iḍā* and *piṅgalā*. *Kapalabhātī* and bandha-tuned breath cycles further clear *nadī* blockages and invigorate *prāṇic* circulation.

Regular and disciplined breathing practice assists one in attaining an ideal of ascetic warrior dedication. This is because it is an assertive approach requiring psychological and physical mastery of one's own energetic field.

In the Tantric worldview, the breath (*prāṇa*) is not merely a biological function but a vector of metaphysical force, a bridge between material and subtle. For Evola, particularly in *The Yoga of Power*, breath control is a form of *kriyā* — action guided by will. It allows a practitioner to assert dominion over his interior world.

Breathing disciplines dissolve the indolence of a conditioned personality to awaken latent energies stored in a subtle body. *Nāḍī-śodhana* and *kapālabhātī* serve as paired techniques of purification and ignition. The former cleanses and balances the pathways; the latter strikes a fire.

Nāḍī-Śodhana (नाड़ी-शोधन) — "Cleansing of the Subtle Channels"

Nāḍī-śodhana (also called *anuloma-viloma*) is a gentle yet powerful practice that purifies subtle energy channels (*nāḍīs*) — specifically *iḍā*, *piṅgalā*, and *suṣumṇā*. These three *nāḍīs* run alongside and within a spinal column and are essential to *kuṇḍalinī yoga*. The *Hatha Yoga Pradīpikā* states:

नाड़ी शुद्धि यथा प्राणा सुषुम्णायां प्रवर्तते।

तदा योगी कुंडलिनी जाग्रति भवति॥

Nāḍī śuddhi yathā prāṇā suṣumṇāyāṁ pravartate
tadā yogī kuṇḍalinī jāgrati bhavati

"When the nāḍīs are purified, the prāṇa flows through the suṣumṇā, and the mind becomes steady. Then the yogī becomes fit for kuṇḍalinī awakening."

In Evolian terms, this exercise reflects a "rectification of the instrument." Just as a sword must be tempered and aligned before wielding, so too the subtle anatomy of man must be equilibrated. Without such balance, spiritual ascent remains unstable or fragmented.

How to perform *Nāḍī-Śodhana*

Posture: Sit in *siddhāsana*, *padmāsana*, or *bhadrāsana* with the spine erect, shoulders relaxed, and eyes closed. Adopt a meditative attitude (*dhāraṇā*).

Hand Mudra: Use the right hand in *viṣṇu mudrā* (index and middle fingers curled inward, thumb and ring finger free). The thumb is used to close the right nostril; the ring finger closes the left.

Breath Cycle (One Round): Close the right nostril with the thumb and inhale slowly through the left nostril (*iḍā*) for a count of 8. Close both nostrils and retain the breath (*antar kumbhaka*) for a count of 8. Release the thumb and exhale slowly through the right nostril (*piṅgalā*) for a count of 8. Now inhale through the right nostril for a count of 8. Retain for 8. Exhale through the left nostril for 8.

Repetitions: Begin with 8 rounds and gradually increase to 12-24 rounds over time.

Effects: The symmetrical alternation between lunar (*iḍā*) and solar (*piṅgalā*) channels restores inner polarity, a foundational principle of Tantric metaphysics emphasized throughout *The Yoga of Power*. Once the *nāḍīs* are clear, *prāṇa* can move into *suṣumṇā*, the vertical axis of transcendence. Mental agitation subsides, allowing an aspirant to approach stillness (*śūnya*) necessary for inner work.

Nāḍī-śodhana should be practiced before *mantra japa*, visualization (*dhyāna*), or any ritual invoking *Śakti*, as it harmonizes and prepares the interior field.

Kapālabhātī (कपालभाति) — "Skull-Illuminating Breath"

Kapālabhātī is classified as a *śatkarman* (purificatory *kriyā*) in Hatha Yoga texts, intended to clear the physical and energetic channels through forced exhalation. Beyond cleansing, it generates heat, stimulates *tapas* (internal fire), and activates the *manipūra cakra*, seat of will (*icchā-śakti*) and solar force.

The *Gheraṇḍa Saṁhitā* describes it thus:

कपालभात्या सर्वरोगा हन्ति शरीरं दीप्यमानं बलवद्भवेत्।

कपालभात्याः फलं सुखप्रदं तस्यारोग्यं प्रलयप्रदं॥

Kapālabhātyā sarvarogā hanti, śarīraṁ dīpyamānaṁ balavadbhavet
Kapālabhātyāḥ phalaṁ sukha-pradaṁ tasyārogyaṁ pralaya-pradaṁ

"Through kapālabhātī all diseases of the body vanish, and the body becomes luminous and strong."

Kapālabhātī is the act of purification through flame. Evola often refers to interior fire — a transformation of lower energies into fuel for ascent. *Kapālabhātī* actualizes this through the body itself, making it a furnace of realization. It is especially suitable for the *Vīra* temperament — vigorous, will-driven, and aspiring toward mastery.

How to perform *Kapālabhātī*

Posture: Sit in a meditative seat with spine upright and face relaxed. Hands rest on knees in *chin mudrā*.

Technique: Inhale passively (allow breath to enter naturally). Exhale actively and sharply by snapping the abdomen inward (using the lower belly muscles). Allow inhalation to follow passively and naturally. Repeat this cycle rhythmically, like a bellows. After 24 exhalations, inhale fully, retain the breath for a few seconds (*kumbhaka*), then exhale slowly and rest.

Precautions: Begin with 1-2 cycles and gradually work up to 4-8 rounds. Perform on an empty stomach and avoid if prone to high blood pressure.

Effects: *Kapālabhātī* "clears the skull" by purging tamasic stagnation and awakening the *prāṇic* field. Active exhalation stimulates the *manipūra cakra*, burns away lethargy, and charges a nervous system with vitality. Its name — "that which makes the skull shine" — is no metaphor; an awakened mind becomes radiant and directed.

In Tantric practice, this prepares an aspirant for deeper *kumbhaka*, bandha work, or an activation of *kuṇḍalinī*. It also instills a state of inner heat (*tapas*) conducive to ritual potency and visualization.

Nāḍī-śodhana and *kapālabhātī* are not mere exercises but sacred operations. They sharpen the will, clear the vessel, and ignite a flame of inward ascent. They are technologies of self-transformation; practices that change one into something more than human (at least by modern standards).

These practices cultivate the solar attitude — a supra-human state of intentional presence needed to walk the path of a Tantric warrior. The breath is no longer merely physiological; it becomes a ritual implement. It is the forge in which a Self (*Ātman*) is remembered and revealed.

Avalon and the *Hatha Yoga Pradīpikā* confirm that purifying *nāḍīs* precedes chakra activation and eventual *kundalinī* ascent. Indeed, only when *iḍā* and *piṅgalā* are in balance does *sūṣumṇā* open fully, allowing the dormant serpent power at *mūlādhāra* to rise. Gopi Krishna's documented challenges with premature *kundalinī* awakening through imbalanced *nāḍīs* attest to this risk. Evola echoes these cautions: a body unconditioned by discipline can become a site of psychic disaster rather than liberation.

From Evola's vantage a body is not an obstacle to be excelled but a structured field to be mastered (*The Yoga of Power*). He regards Hatha Yoga as a strategic staging ground — an armor of stillness and energy enabling practitioners to approach Tantric rites as lords of their internal domains. The physical discipline precedes and underpins sacred ritual, ensuring stability amid high-transformative energies.

The following Tantric *Hatha Sādhana* routine synthesizes these principles:

1. Morning Cleansing and Posture Practice (Āṣana): Begin in *siddhāsana* with spine erect. Practice *padmāsana* and *bhuadhrāsana* to stabilize pelvic and spine axis. Maintain awareness on energetic alignment.

2. Bandha Activation: With eyes closed, engage the *mūla bandha* (contract perineum), then *uḍḍiyāna bandha* (draw the abdomen). Hold each lock for several breaths, pulling energy inward and upward.

3. Prāṇāyāma Practice: Perform 8 minutes of *nāḍī-śodhana*, keeping exhalation equal to inhalation. Visualize clearing white (*iḍā*) and red (*piṅgalā*) energies. Follow with *kapalabhātī* for 48 breaths to energize the *nadī* network.

4. Mudrā Activation: Adopt *chin mudrā* (thumb and index touch with palms on knees). Maintain posture. Each finger seals mental aspects and stabilizes the *prāṇa* loop.

5. Breath-Mantra Synchronization: Engage in silent mantra with breaths: inhale "*Om*," exhale "*Hroum.*" Envision vibratory energy traveling up the center channel, strengthening the subtle body's structural matrix.

6. Meditation and Energy Integration: Sit in stillness. Sense subtle movement in spine and chest. Visualize a sphere of inner light radiating at the *ajñā* chakra. Anchor awareness there for 2-4 minutes.

7. Closing Sequence: Release bandhas slowly. Apply *khecarī mudrā* (tongue pressed upon one's soft palate) for a few minutes to allow energy to settle. Walk in silence for assimilation.

8. Daily Integration: Through the day, maintain presence at the heart and head centers. Let action be guided by an open center, rather than instigated by reactive impulses.

The *Shiva Samhitā* explicitly depicts the body as a cosmic temple, with the spine as Mount Meru, surrounded by rivers (*nāḍīs*), seas (chakras), and divine shrines (subtle centers). Evola would interpret this as intentional magical geography, enacted through physical discipline, ritual, and inner governance.

The adept learns to orient properly within their own bodily universe. This principally occurs not at its surface, but within its subtle infrastructure. One's body should not be ignored, but purified, mastered, and consecrated.

Through Hatha Yoga, *prāṇāyāma*, *bandha*, and *mudrā*, the body-as-sacred vessel becomes a realm of self-rulership. It is a place where cosmic principle and sovereign purpose converge. By honoring its form and commanding its energies, an adept reclaims physical existence as both a vehicle for transcendence and an embodiment of Tradition.

The Great Seal of Union and Transcendence

Mahāmudrā (literally translated as "The Great Seal") is one of the most advanced and potent practices in both Hatha Yoga and Tantra. It is a multidimensional — hybrid psychological, spiritual, and physiological — technique designed to seal or lock-in awakened energies generated through a well-organized practice, including an alchemical charge of sexual rites such as Maithuna. *Mahāmudrā's* purpose is to inwardly unite spiritual power, bringing the vitality of existence under a jurisdiction of sovereign will and refined awareness.

Scriptural sources and commentaries from Avalon and the Hatha Yoga texts emphasize that *mahāmudrā* serves to seal activated energy within one's subtle body. According to these sources, performing the *mahāmudrā* after *kumabaka* (breath retention) or other enflaming ritual action ensures energy does not dissipate downward into physical or psychological realms. Instead, it is absorbed upward through one's central channel (*suṣumnā-nāḍī*) and toward heightened consciousness. This both purifies subtle channels and empowers a practitioner to sustain deep meditative states.

Without such intentional sealing, forces stirred within one's body risk weakening or dispersing, particularly during moments of heightened physiological arousal. *Mahāmudrā* functions as a final act of sovereign interiorization. Evola, especially in *The Yoga of Power*, viewed spiritual practice as a deliberate act of inner consolidation. It is one bringing the volatile energies of life, including eros, under the direction of True Will and Higher Intellect (*buddhi*).

Mahāmudrā, then, becomes a synthesis of embodiment and metaphysics. The practitioner holds and transmits energy not outwardly, but inwardly, stabilizing an inner axis (*merudanda*) and integrating all experiences into a center of stillness and transcendence.

In Tantric Hatha Yoga, as per *Gheranda Samhita* and *Hatha Yoga Pradipika*, *mahāmudrā* is said to destroy all defects and purify the *nāḍīs* (subtle channels), enabling the practitioner to progress toward liberation (*moksha*). It is also described in Avalon's *The Serpent Power* as a key seal to retain the upward-moving *kundalinī* energy once it has been awakened, ensuring it does not dissipate downward into lower chakras or exit through the sensory field.

The active term "*mudrā*" here refers to a "seal," "gesture," or "energetic lock." In *mahāmudrā*, this notable concept is taken to its fullest extent. All energy (*prāṇa*), awareness (*citta*), and desire (*kāma*) are drawn inward, directed upward, and sealed within a practitioner's being.

The symbolism is especially potent. When performed after Maithuna or deep meditation, *mahāmudrā* is said to seal within the body union of Shiva and Shakti. *Prāṇic* energy created from breath, posture, and eros is held, sublimated, and transformed into higher awareness. It is precisely this sort of transcendental virility which Evola regarded as a mark of the *Vīra* — a Tantric spiritual warrior.

Mahāmudrā is indispensable within sexual tantric rites such as Maithuna. It transforms the energy generated during union into a vehicle for spiritual refinement. Sexual fluid is retained, not expelled, and inner channels are sealed so that resonance remains internal rather than dissipating externally. In non-sexual spiritual disciplines, *mahāmudrā* still plays a vital role; it is a final stage in sequences of pranayama, meditation, mantra, and mudra — serving as an energetic "capstone."

Effects of *mahāmudrā* are both energetic and psychological. Practitioners often report an enhancement in their capacity to remain unmoved by external distractions, cultivating resilient equanimity and a stable, rooted internal axis. This reflects the quintessentially Evolian ideal of a differentiated individual who remains sovereign even amid decline. Far from being passive, the practice refines instinctual force into conscious spiritual potency, transforming raw energies into *ojas*: the subtle fuel of presence and will.

Mastery of *mahāmudrā* requires intense preparation. Classic texts and Tantric authorities caution against engaging in this practice prematurely. Mastery of associated skills like personal growth, psychic grounding, spiritual discipline (asana, breath control, etc.), and emotional maturity are essential. The practice should be undertaken progressively, ideally under guidance or rigorous self-discipline that honors lineage and standards of transmission.

Technically, practice involves seated posture — commonly with one leg folded and the other extended — combined with deep inhalation, *jālandhara bandha* (chin lock), *mūla bandha* (pelvic lock), and *uḍḍiyāna bandha* (abdominal lock), followed by breath retention (*kumbhaka*). During, a practitioner focuses consciousness on one's spinal axis, visualizing *kundalinī* energy rising toward the crown. Upon release, one exhales slowly while discharging each lock gently in reverse sequence.

Repetition of this sequence four to eight times, ideally after serious energetic or spiritual work, further stabilizes energy in the higher centers. Over time, this practice yields profound clarity, emotional stability, and energetic resilience.

How to Perform *Mahāmudrā* (Traditional Technique)

Posture: Sit on the ground with the left leg extended straight in front. Fold the right leg so that the heel presses into the perineum (similar to *Siddhāsana*). Keep the spine erect and the gaze slightly downward toward the heart center or tip of the nose. This posture creates pressure at the *mūlādhāra* (root chakra), preventing downward dissipation of energy.

Breath Control and Internal Locks: Inhale deeply through both nostrils. Apply *Jālandhara Bandha* (chin lock) by pressing the chin firmly against the chest at the clavicle notch. Retain the breath (*kumbhaka*), and simultaneously apply *Mūla Bandha* (pelvic floor lock), contracting the perineum to draw energy upward, and *Uḍḍiyāna Bandha* (abdominal lock), pulling the abdomen inward and upward toward the spine. These three bandhas seal energy within the central channel (*suṣumnā-nāḍī*).

Awareness and Visualization: Focus mental attention on the spine or along the *suṣumnā*. Visualize the *kundalinī śakti* rising upward toward the *sahasrāra* (crown chakra). Intone the *bīja* sound "*Om.*"

Release: After several seconds (or minutes, as capability increases), exhale slowly while releasing all three bandhas in reverse order. Switch legs and repeat the process on the other side. Ideally, perform 4-8 rounds per session.

Uses: Apply *mahāmudrā* after meditation or *prāṇāyāma,* and following Maithuna or other forms of high-energy ritual. It can be utilized as a final step in a series of Tantric or yogic practices, or a self-contained *sādhanā* for sealing and refining energy.

In the context of Maithuna, *mahāmudrā* is essential to avoid energetic dissipation. By retaining and re-directing energy freed or at least stimulated during a ritual, one transforms potential bindu (seminal or energetic essence) into *ojas* — the subtle fuel of spiritual ascent. Practitioners over time report better clarity and insight, enhanced bodily control and stillness, heightened meditation (*dhyāna*), erotic refinement and sexual sublimation, emotional equilibrium, and a greater resistance to distraction and decay. All this echoes Evola's principle of inner fortification amid external dissolution.

In short, *mahāmudrā* seals not only energy, but also resolve. It is the yogic signature of someone who chooses mastery over surrender, transformation over indulgence, and inner ascent over outer dissipation. In the broader Tantric and Traditionalist framework, *mahāmudrā* exemplifies the talent of transcendence through internal control and somatic application.

It affirms the body not as an obstacle, but as a vessel and instrument for realizing the Absolute (*Paramātman*). It seals the currents of life, redirects vital erotic force upward, and makes a practitioner not a mere observer of sacred reality, but its living epitome. For those Tantrically treading the path of aristocratic spirituality, of "riding the tiger" and conquering the world from within, *mahāmudrā* is not optional but essential.

Mahāmudrā is a transformative seal that preserves inner potency, anchors a subtle field, and enables awakened presence within the world. It exemplifies the Tantric master's method: disciplined form wielded as a bearer of transcendent force. For those following a way of spiritual sovereignty, *mahāmudrā* is both a culminating symbol and living technique. It is a ritual gesture in which time, energy, and consciousness converge under the aegis of inner authority.

Man and His Becoming

In the *Katha Upaniṣad*, Nachiketa is told of a fire within:

अङ्गुष्ठमात्रः पुरुषो मध्य आत्मनि तिष्ठति

Aṅguṣṭhamātraḥ puruṣo madhya ātmani tiṣṭhati

"The Purusha, of the size of a thumb, dwells in the body."

This Purusha is also described as a "smokeless flame" — an inner spark superior to gross existence. This flame is individual Self (*Ātman*): conscious, timeless, and luminous, pervading the myriad subtleties of human form. It is a microcosmic reflection of Brahman, mirroring the cosmic Self underlying all.

Guénon writes man can be understood as twofold: a temporal individual (*jīva*, ego-bound) and eternal person (*pudgala* or "personality"), which is still yet a limited expression of the Supreme Self (*Paramātmā*). Evola translates this into his terms: ego (*ahaṅkāra*) is a machine of conditioning, while Self (*ātman*) is a sovereign witness and lord of the internal realm.

In this reading Purusha relates to *Śiva*, a transcendent subject. *Prakṛti*, as matrix of manifestation, is *Śakti*, the energizing substance. Man's existence is a bridge connecting manifest world (*Prakṛti*) with unmanifest ground (*Purusha*).

Guénon's distinction between "personality" (a supreme and permanent Self) and "individual" (dynamic, egoic personality) is metaphysically precise. Personality corresponds to the eternal *Atma*: unconditioned Self. An individual is an egoic vehicle born of *Prakṛti's* interplay of the three *guṇas*: *sattva*, *rajas*, and *tamas*.

Evola reframes this dialectic as a vertical drive of the Tantric adept. The individual must train their egoic functions without annihilation, preserving them as instruments of transcendent will and divine consciousness.

Arthur Avalon's *Serpent Power* presents the classical schema of *koshas*, *nadis*, and *chakras*. The *suṣumnā-nādī* is a central axis; *īḍā* and *piṅgalā* are lunar and solar currents. *Kuṇḍalinī-śakti* coils at the base (*mūlādhāra*) awaiting activation.

Avalon outlines how these channels align with the subtle sheaths (*koshas*): from *annamayī* (physical) through *prāṇamayī* (vital), *manomayī* (mental), *vijñānamayī* (intellectual), to *ānandamayī* (bliss). *Kundalinī's* ascent activates each chakra (*cakra-karpura-spanda*) purifying and integrating body, breath, mind, intelligence, and enjoyment.

Guénon describes a subtle channel passing from the left ventricle of the heart to the pineal gland, and ending in the middle of the brain. This is the seat of the Spiritual Sun (*Āditya*). He cites the *Yājñavalkya Upaniṣad*, affirming:

"The Golden Sun is in the middle; he is this Ātman, without evil, without fear."

This channel corresponds to the *ajñā-cakra*. An adept accessing it via *pranayama*, *nyāsa*, and *dhyana* enters the Solar Ray of Brahman, attaining illumined awareness.

Both the *Katha* and Guénon's commentary speak of a smokeless fire within at the heart-center, glowing like a celestial flame. It is the spiritual ignition of consciousness awakened through yogic discipline. Guénon uses coronal artery imagery to suggest that via subtle channels one may access a Spiritual Sun at the head (equivalent to the Third Eye) offering direct vision into a transcendental Self.

Practical Evolian-Tantric Application

Establishing awareness of Purusha: Begin with meditation on Katha's flame. Sit in *siddhāsana*, place awareness in the center of the chest, visualize a smokeless flame, repeating the mantra: "*Puruṣhāsmallatulyahaṃ*." This aligns awareness with a transcendental Self rather than one's ego.

Breath and Subtle Channel Activation: Practice alternate nostril breathing while holding the mind steady on the heart's flash. Visualize *prāṇa* ascending through *nāḍīs* into the heart, then the pineal. At the same time intone the *bija* "*Om*" internally with the inhalation, aligning subtle breath with cosmic sound.

Third-Eye Invocation: Once prana reaches the pineal center, visualize it as a solar disc, golden and still. Recite an *Ajñācakra* mantra (e.g. "*Om hṛīm*") to settle awareness there. Contemplate the Spiritual Sun — intense and shining without flame.

Microcosmic-Macrocosmic Convergence: Recognize the presence of Brahma/Supreme Self within the heart and third eye. Let this awareness reflect outward, perceiving everyday phenomena as expressions of the same Self.

Integration into Daily Life: Approach obligations with an awareness of the third-eye witness. This is disciplined presence in action. Perform it with precision, not egoistic reactivity.

Purusha is unchanging and radiant Self; *Prakṛti* is its vehicle as a dynamic, substantiated world. An adept navigates the world using a microcosmic structure of his own subtle body. An adept imposes hierarchical order upon internal chaos, cultivating the sovereignty of consciousness.

The "smokeless flame" metaphor recurs in both Veda and Tantra, symbolizing an inner fire of alchemical transformation. The coronal spiritual ray accessed via the third eye is a merger-point, a vertical axis where microcosm meets macrocosm. Here, *ātma-vidyā* (self-knowledge) translates to spiritual authority.

The relationship between man and his becoming is a twofold journey: rousing vertical realization (*Purusha*) and assuming sovereignty over one's inner structure (*koshas*, *chakras*, solar ray). Metaphysical insight and warrior ethos synchronize into a paradigm demanding rigor, precision, and internal discipline.

A Tantric adept is an architect of his becoming. Building from the core flame to crowned solar witness, he is constructing an adamantine body while achieving self-rule. He is likewise impressing Tradition upon body, mind, and spirit.

Tantric Cosmology

Tantric cosmology begins with *Param-Śiva*, the Supreme Absolute — an undivided and unmovable principle of pure being beyond name, form, or causality. In the Shaivite Tantric tradition (particularly as articulated in the Kashmiri and Kaula schools) *Param-Śiva* manifests the universe through a self-limiting act, bifurcating into two essential poles: *Śiva* as pure consciousness (*cit*) and *Śakti* as creative force (*śakti*).

This initial polarity is not a duality in the ordinary sense but a metaphysical pair — *Śiva* remaining transcendently still, while *Śakti* brings forth the cosmos in movement. From this division arises an intricate sequence of thirty-six *tattvas* or ontological principles, describing a descent from pristine consciousness to unrefined materiality. Evola interprets this not as a fall, but a necessary process an initiate must willfully reverse.

The first layer of this metaphysical descent is *māyā*, veil of illusion or differentiation giving rise to the five *kañchukas* or limitations. They are made of *kāla* (time), *niyati* (causality), *vidyā* (limited knowledge), *kalā* (limited agency), and *rāga* (desire or attachment). These cloak infinite self, producing an experience of *puruṣa* (limited individual consciousness) distinguished from *prakṛti* (dynamic material substratum of the universe).

From here, the tattvas unfold into elements of cognition and embodiment: *buddhi* (intellect), *ahaṅkāra* (ego), *manas* (mind), the ten *indriyas* (sense and action faculties), and finally *pañca bhūtas*, the five gross elements: earth, water, fire, air, and ether. Each element corresponds not only to a physical substance, but vibrational archetypes and *bija* mantras. Earth (*pṛthvī*) is linked to the mantra "*Lam*" and one's sense of smell; water (*jala*) corresponds with "*Vam*" and taste; fire (*agni*) is associated with "*Ram*" and sight; air (*vāyu*) is tied to "*Yam*" and touch; ether (*ākāśa*) is connected with "*Ham*" and sound. These *bija* mantras are used in *nyāsa* (placement) practices, where a practitioner installs each element into a corresponding energy center or chakra.

The five elements are not inert matter, but energies that can be accessed, purified, and directed. The *sādhaka* (aspirant) ritually purifies each element through *bhūta-śuddhi* (elemental purification), preparing a subtle body for *kundalinī* awakening.

The upward path from manifested elements back to *Param-Śiva* is enacted through yogic discipline. Coiled like a serpent, *kundalini* — as described in both Tantric texts and Eliade's *Yoga: Immortality and Freedom* — lies dormant in the *mūlādhāra* chakra at the base of a spine. Through practices such as *prāṇāyāma* (breath control), *bandha* (locks), *mudrā* (gestures), and mantra repetition, a practitioner stimulates *kundalinī* to rise through the *suṣumnā nāḍī*, passing through each chakra and dissolving tattvas layer by layer till uniting with *Śiva* in a *sahasrāra* (thousand-petalled lotus) at the crown of the head.

This cosmology is not abstract speculation — it is a living configuration through which an adept engages the world. In practical terms, a daily Tantric ritual begins with physical and mental purification: cleansing the body, stabilizing posture, and controlling the breath. This is followed by *pañca-bhūta nyāsa*, where a practitioner invokes each element using its associated mantra and visualizes its energy stabilizing and activating the corresponding chakra.

The earth element is visualized at the base of the spine while intoning "*Lam*," establishing groundedness and strength. Water is called into the pelvic region with "*Vam*," invoking fluidity and adaptability. Fire is brought into the solar plexus with "*Ram*," awakening transformative will. Air is placed in the heart center with "*Yam*," refining emotional energy and preparing it for higher sublimation. Ether is installed in the throat with "*Ham*," attuning a practitioner to subtle resonance and expression. These placements activate an elemental structure of the self, turning one's body into a ritual field.

After elemental invocation, a practitioner meditates upon the *Śiva-Śakti* polarity, invoking *Śiva* through "*Oṁ namaḥ Śivāya*" and *Śakti* through "*Oṁ Hrīṁ Śrīṁ Klīṁ*." These are energetic keys aligning an individual or couple with cosmic forces. *Kundalinī* is guided upward through breath and visualization, gradually burning through veils of ego, desire, and duality. The goal is to dissolve a limited self into unconditioned Absolute. This is not mere mystical absorption, but the recovery of *ātma-jñāna:* self-knowledge as an essence of being.

Evola interprets this entire process as an expression of the warrior's path. In both *Ride the Tiger* and *Yoga of Power*, he rejects any sentimental or escapist approach to spirituality. Instead, he views Tantra as a method of actively engaging the world's forces, transmuting them through discipline and inner command. A spiritual adept is not a mystic lost in formlessness but a conscious, virile center of will: an agent of transcendence. He harnesses elemental powers not for pleasure or dissolution, but ascesis — a burning away of dross to reveal the Self.

The elements themselves can be used as powers in daily life. Earth energy cultivates grounded decisiveness. Water deepens a positive adaptability. Fire fuels ambition and inner heat (tapas). Air elevates one's thoughts and emotions. Ether provides clarity and spiritual presence.

These become extensions of one's higher will when ritually purified and integrated. In this sense, the practitioner reenacts a cosmogenesis of the universe through ritual, only in reverse. In doing so, one retraces the steps of creation back to their source in *Param-Śiva*.

At the conclusion of the ritual, an adept performs *antarāṅga* (inner closing), stabilizing the energy through inverted postures or mantric sealing. The state of meditative stillness that follows is lucid awareness — *samādhi* as grounded sovereignty. Mantras such as "*Śivoham*" ("I am Śiva") or "*Aham Brahmāsmi*" ("I am the Absolute") are not affirmed as fanciful views, but acknowledged as viscerally apprehended states of being.

Tantric cosmology thus provides a structured metaphysical and practical map for self-overcoming. Evola's interpretation situates it within a warrior's ethos, one that refuses passivity and demands inner mastery. The descent of *Param-Śiva* into form is not a fall to be lamented, but a reality to be transformed through ritual, will, and alignment.

The Shaivite Tantric practitioner reclaims this descent by deliberately reversing it, turning body and cosmos into a ladder of ascent. This is the essence of Evola's magical idealism: that consciousness rightly engaged and directed does not reflect reality. Instead it shapes, masters, and transcends it.

The Alchemy of Desire

Desire unfolds within Tantra as a profound transformative technique converting raw sensual energy into potent spiritual power. Drawing upon Evola's outlook in *Eros and the Mysteries of Love*, erotic desire is elevated as a metaphorical bridge — an existential impulse temporarily dissolving the ego-boundary, aiming to reclaim an original unity with the divine.

Evola highlights a metaphysical dimension of eros as a form of sacred longing that, when disciplined, becomes a catalyst for transcendence rather than spiritual descent. Tantra's Left-Hand Path (*Vāmācāra*) uses controlled, often taboo expressions of desire within ritual contexts. *The Yoga of Power* presents *Vāmācāra* as a method for confronting and mastering sexual energy rather than repressing it.

Such practices conventionally involve ritualized use of the "Five Ms" (*pañcamakāra*) — wine, meat, fish, grain, intercourse — in a structured, sacred framework. It is a fiercely disciplined path. One enters the realm of desire with unwavering *icchā-śuddhi* (purity of intent), not from indulgence but sovereignty.

Evola warns in *Ride the Tiger* that without rigorous self-discipline, desire can easily derail a practitioner into hedonistic attachment. Ritual use of desire is ethical only when framed by clear intention, ascetic boundaries, and conscious leadership of the will. The *Vāmācāra* adept must always preserve awareness as an immovable *Śiva*-like axis while energetically engaging Shakti through symbolic or actual rites. The body and senses become tools, not masters.

Psycho-physiological exercises help one sublimate desire. Hatha Yoga and breath discipline prepare a subtle body for transformative currents. Practices such as *prāṇāyāma*, bandhas, and *kundalinī* activation align vitality for higher channeling.

In *The Serpent Power*, Avalon underscores visualization techniques and seed-mantra internalization as methods to transmute lower impulses into rising spiritual fire. Meticulous practice of *nyāsa* and subtle mental imagery fosters internal restructuring, projecting an initiate's intentions onto sacred geometry rather than simply experiencing profane sensation.

One method involves the following sequence. Commence with *prāṇāyāma* and *banda* to still the mind and seal subtle currents. Use visualization to see desire as *Saṅkara's* Shakti, coiled and potent.

Recite a mantra such as "*Klim*" or "*Hrīm*" while maintaining *ekāgratā* (one-pointedness). Move through intentional sexual intercourse (*maithuna*) as a ritualized dyad where breath, eye contact, and intonation align in a single energetic stream.

To ensure effective practice, certain disciplines are essential:

- Physical cleansing each morning and before ritual.

- *Mantra japa* (108 repetitions) of *bija* like *klīm* or *hrīm* in a consecrated space, ideally with a *rudrākṣa* mala and established *sankalpa* (intentional vow).
- Dietary moderation (principally consuming healthy, nourishing, unprocessed foods), avoiding inebriants and pollutants that diminish vital force, and fasting at least two hours prior to ritual or other practices.
- Emotional vigilance (noting reactions while limiting impulsivity) and generally taming one's passions.

Evola highlights the symbolic significance of eros as tension between the "*black steed and white steed*" (representing instinct and spirit) being driven by a chariot of the soul. This alchemical interplay fuels tapas (inner heat) when an initiate retains *virya* and resists letting urge disseminate his awareness.

Developing a discipline of desire preserves integrity. Evola decries both repression and indulgence. He clarifies how proper usage of eros requires viewing it as magical energy, not sensual experience. Through discipline, eros becomes a way awareness can reshape its own psychic structure — and in turn ecosystem.

Evola frames this as a strategy of austere sexuality, stressing how yearning itself is not a goal; its alchemical transmutation into power and lucidity is the aim. Practitioners who sincerely follow this path overcome longing, not gratify it. They become masters of Shakti rather than subjects to it.

Craving thus becomes an alchemical flame purifying egoic lead into a gold of presence. Evola's worldview highlights how Tantra is not a path of indulgence, but a martial strategy for inner sovereignty. Desire is engaged knowingly, disciplined rigorously, and sublimated into an enduring flame of ascension. Sexuality is elevated to an integration of self with Absolute.

A brief framework for a paired ritual (*maithuna*), attested in *Kaula* and *Trika* lineages and amenable to an Evolian framing, may be structured as follows:

Initial Preparation (Pūrvakarman): *Śaucam* (purification) — bathing, silence, and ritual fasting. Assume an *āsana* (e.g., *siddhāsana*), performing *nāḍī śodhana* for 24 cycles.

Mantra invocation: "*Oṁ namaḥ Śivāya*" invoking the axis of consciousness; "*Oṁ Hrīṁ Śrīṁ Klim*" invoking Shakti's power.

Main Ritual (Mukhya Karman): Visualize the partner as divine Shakti — not as simply a woman, but *śakti-tattva*. Chant the *Śiva-Śakti Dhyāna*:

शिवं शान्तं जगत्कारणं भवं भवाभावमात्मकम् ।

शक्तिं चानन्तशक्तिं च ध्यायामि हृदयाख्यया ॥

Śivaṁ śāntaṁ jagatkāraṇaṁ bhavaṁ bhavābhāvamātmakam
Śaktiṁ cānantaśaktiṁ ca dhyāyāmi hr̥diyākhyayā

"I meditate upon Śiva, the cause of the world, the peaceful one, beyond becoming and non-becoming; and upon Śakti, the infinite power, through the inner heart."

Enter sacred union (*maithuna*), maintaining *ekāgratā* (one-pointed awareness). Recite the *"Hrīṁ-Klim" bīja* mantra. Imagine *Śiva* seated in *sahasrāra* with Shakti, both rising upward.

Close (Uttarāṅga): Uncouple and sit facing one another in an *āsana* while chanting the *Guru Gāyatrī*:

ॐ अज्ञानातिमिरान्धस्य ज्ञानाञ्जनशलाकया ।

चक्षुरुन्मीलितं येन तस्मै श्रीगुरवे नमः ॥

Om ajñānātimirāndhasya jñānāñjanaśalākayā |
Cakṣurunmīlitaṁ yena tasmai śrīgurave namaḥ ||

"I offer my salutations to that Supreme Guru, who, by the application of the salve of wisdom, has removed the darkness of ignorance from my eyes, and has opened my vision."

Perform *mahāmudrā*, then rest in *dhyāna* for an interval.

Intent, boundaries, and heroism are stressed through Evola's work. An adept is not a slave to desire nor denialist, but an actor in the theater of transformation. Longing is confronted — it is acknowledged and refined, not suppressed or indulged.

The alchemy of desire transmutes eros into transcendence. Body becomes a crucible, the senses phials, and consciousness a transforming fire. Once sublimated, desire is a blazing torch guiding to higher ground. This is the Tantra of warriors: a path where raw appetite is burned away leaving only being.

Chakras and the Serpent Power

Kundalinī is latent *śakti*: coiled energy seated at the base of the spine and identified with the goddess's dormant power. When awakened through Tantric *sādhana*, this energy ascends via a central channel (*suṣumnā nāḍī*), piercing successive chakras to unite with *Śiva* in the *sahasrāra*, culminating in apotheotic transcendence. Avalon describes *kundalinī* as "latent divinity... the power that transforms man into the gods." This ascent is an expression of inner sovereignty, where disciplined perception consciously dismantles limitations, reversing a cosmic descent of tattvas to soar the heights of higher awareness.

The chakra system serves as a cartography of this ascent. Though differing in number across traditions, a seven-chakra model remains prominent. Each is a psycho-spiritual nexus and node of energy, perception, and expansion. From *mūlādhāra* (grounded will) at base to *svādhiṣṭhāna* (creative flow) in the lower torso, *maṇipūra* (transformative fire) at plexus, *anāhata* (imbued compassion) at heart, *viśuddha* (vocal resonance) in the throat, to *ajāna* (inner vision) at brow, culminating in *sahasrāra* (pure knowing), each center is a milestone toward awakening.

Voice, vision, and will: the ancient *Upaniṣads* provide initial wisdom on controlling subtle energetic ascent. In the *Katha Upanishad* one finds the declaration "from that [Self] the light illumines all" — a statement pointing to an inward illumination arising as *kundalinī* reaches one's crown. Similarly, *Chandogya* declares "wisdom above the person is real wisdom," conveying a transcendence achieved beyond ego-bound awareness. This describes exactly the summit of *kundalinī* ascent.

Eliade warns of dangers inherent in premature activation. In *Yoga: Immortality and Freedom*, he recounts initiates who suffered mental and physiological unbalance from unprepared *kundalinī* eruptions. He advises preparatory disciplines: breath control, elemental cleansing (*bhūta-śuddhi*), mental focus, and grounding as necessary pre-conditions for ascent.

The serpent motif runs deep across Indo-European myth. Ouroboros in Greek alchemy is venom and wisdom embodied. The Vedic *sarpa* reveals a serpent's ambivalence as poisonous, but enlightening when mastered. This incongruity likely reflects an older, pre-Aryan substratum in the Indic mythos (probably invoking the Indus Valley's reverence for female serpent deities) incorporated into later Hindu Tantra as a symbol of both creation and ruin, reflective of *Śakti's* dual aspect.

Avalon emphasizes a serpent is "the primal spiritual force" dormant in man, neither good nor evil until willfully engaged. Evola views it as a core of virile power: raw energy that yields sovereignty when disciplined through ritual, awareness, and metaphysical integration.

Kundalinī is Tantric power in concentrated form. The chakra system maps its inner terrain. An actionable style frames the ascent as a deliberate exercise in reclaiming sovereignty over a fallen and fragmented self. The Indo-European serpent motif illustrates its archetypal gravity.

A practical *kundalinī*-raising ritual designed around Tantric insights and Traditional safeguards may be described as:

Preparation (Pūrvakarman): The practitioner bathes, consecrates the space, and establishes an intention (*saṃkalpa*). Seated in a stable meditative posture (e.g., *siddhāsana*), silence and inner receptivity are established.

Bhūta-Śuddhi & Prāṇāyāma: The adept performs *mūlādhāra*, *ūḍīyāṇī*, and *jalāṃdhāra* bandhas while engaging in slow, circular breathing. This unblocks gross energies, channeling vital force into the central pathway to increase in subtlety while rising.

Element and Bīja Invocation: Each chakra is activated via its visualization and *bija mantra*.

Mūlādhāra — a crimson square and mantra of *Lam*.

Svādhiṣṭhāna — an ochre pillar and mantra of *Vam*.

Maṇipūra — a gold disc and mantra of *Ram*.

Anāhata — an emerald triangle (upward) and mantra of *Yam*.

Viśuddha — a navy triangle (downward) and mantra of *Ham*.

Ajña — an indigo diamond (horizontal) and mantra of *Om*.

Sahasrāra — an ivory crown and mantra of *Hroum*.

The practitioner mentally places each mantra in its chakra, feeling its resonance and stabilizing the subtle centers. This is central to elemental purification and chakra activation.

Kundalinī Invocation (Kriyā): Reciting the mantra "*Om hrīm klīm,*" attention is focused on the *mūlādhāra.* One visualizes a serpent uncoiling and ascending with each breath, entering the next chakra, while mantra supports gradual movement upward.

Summit Realization: When the serpent reaches *ajāna,* light and inner sound are experienced. Upon entry into *sahasrāra, jīva* dissolves into *Śiva* consciousness. A practitioner remains in a lucid state like the *chidakāśa,* witnessing absolute awareness — mirroring *ahaṃ brahmāsmi* realization.

Closure (Uttarāṅga): The flow is gently guided back through the chakras via visualization while reciting "Om," re-grounding energy. A concluding affirmation, such as "*Śivoham,*" is recited.

Sealing Presence: Stillness follows. No abstract narrating or logical debriefing is needed. Abiding in luminous detachment, feel the ascent embedding into somatic consciousness.

When ritual is done properly — with respect, readiness, and control — the serpent ascends and an adept becomes a locus of *Śiva* consciousness. That is Tantric initiation in flesh and bone: a transformative union of consciousness and energy, charted through a body's subtle geography and governed by higher will.

Gurus and Inner Guidance

In traditional Tantra, the Guru is far more than an instructor or mentor. He is a conduit through which *Śakti* — transformative power of realization — is transmitted to a disciple's subtle body. Eliade emphasizes in *Yoga: Immortality and Freedom* that the presence of a realized master is vital for helping initiates confront and integrate the deep currents that lie beneath ordinary consciousness. He warns that without proper guidance, attempts at awakening *kundalinī* or engaging in ritual work can unleash overwhelming forces beyond the disciple's control.

For Guénon, a guru performs a recognized role within a traditional lineage, carrying authority of an unbroken chain of initiation. This lineage transmits not only teachings but also spiritual influence (*baraka*), rendering practice effective. A guru's voice imbues disciples with an energetic empowerment that textual study cannot provide. The guru-disciple connection is literal, ritual, and supra-rational. It establishes a spiritual filiation through which a disciple is reborn — a "second birth" — rooted in the deep frames of tradition and structure.

True traditional gurus are rare, especially in the modern West. Aspirants must become "differentiated" — independent, yet rooted. This emphasizes cultivating higher internal guidance (an "inner guru") when no external figure is available.

Become yourself and find your supreme identity within. This means developing faculties of acumen, courage, and self-rule in an absence of formal authority. Such an "inner guru" is realized through continuous awareness, discipline, and alignment with principles inherited from Tradition.

Guénon issues strong caution: not all who call themselves gurus are genuine. A true guru is firmly embedded in a specific tradition, properly authorized, and operates within a recognized succession. Any teacher who offers spiritual authority without recognized lineage or who disregards ritual structure is suspect. Guénon further distinguishes between an outer guru — a visible teacher — and inner guru, which he equates with a transcendent Self (*Paramātmā*) that resides within each being.

When a guru is absent or unavailable, Guénon holds to the necessity of connecting through reverse discourse: reading and study, internalizing sacred forms, and aligning ritual practice within the frames of a tradition. This allows a disciple to open to an inner guru through study and introspective integration.

Begin reading sacred texts — *Upaniṣads*, Tantric scriptures, *dīkṣā* mantras — not informally, but with solemnity, dedication, and focus. Evola admires those who confront chaos internally: warriors who take responsibility for self-transformation. Study not for novelty, but induction. The act of dedicated, ritualized scholarship in silence creates an interior environment where the inner guru may appear.

Set aside daily time for reflective silence. Breathe slowly in a meditative posture. Affirm a *saṅkalpa* like, "May this technique encourage my inner guide."

Gaze inward and listen to subtle insights. The differentiated man must "make oneself central," anchoring to a sacred space within. Consistent self-remembering — in other words, catching the ego's drifting — is essential.

Record insights, challenges, and moments of clarity. Evola notes that "being oneself" requires discovering an inner law. Journaling clarifies this law and reveals patterns, turning inner friction into subtle form — an inner temple for the guru-self to take root.

Engage with peers loyal to Tradition, as these conversations sharpen discernment. It is imperative when communicating with others to emphasize the necessity for appropriate perspective. Discussing texts, concepts, or practices helps maintain rigor and tests personal intuition against Tradition's structure.

This ritual can be practiced even without a physical guru, since it draws upon Tradition's forms:

Morning Purification and Saṅkalpa: Cleanse physically, then light incense and a candle. Silently affirm, "I consecrate my day by aligning with the inner guide: wise, orderly, sovereign."

Text Study and Invocation: Read short verses from an *Upaniṣadic* or Tantric text. For illustration: "*Yo'ham Śivoham*" (योऽहम् शिवोऽहम्) — "I am that, I am Śiva." Touch heart, then brow.

Meditation and Insight: Sit in a stable posture, eyes closed. Focus awareness on breath. Continue for 4-8 minutes, noting emerging intuitive statements ("inner instructions"). Make no judgments — just observe and record later.

Journaling: Immediately after, write down any insights. Over time, patterns clarify the nature of your inner guidance and its orientation clarity.

Weekly Peer Reflection: Once a week, discuss a passage or insight with a trusted peer and fellow seeker. Confirm whether your intuition aligns with Tradition's spiritual laws.

Guénon warns against self-initiation detached from any Tradition — spiritual progress requires context, not novelty. Evola similarly critiques theoretical fantasties or self-directed mysticism. Yet both recognize the grim reality that Traditional structures have collapsed, compelling seekers to build inner edifices anchored in symbolic and metaphysical forms.

The inner guru is not a replacement for Tradition, but a temporary proxy — a living extension of Tradition within the soul — until an authentic initiator appears. Ritual, study, and disciplined self-formation become a magical field where inner authority and subtle direction can emerge and anchor the being.

The inner guru merges two imperatives: pursuit of Tradition and awakening of conscious sovereignty. When authentic gurus are scarce, a serious practitioner should study with reverence, clarity, and structure. He must meditate deeply to reveal latent inner authority, journal to record patterns and develop personal coherence, and *always* check his acumen against Tradition.

This is not populist self-help, but an inner initiation process that invokes hierarchy and a call for differentiation. The inner guru manifests through a disciplined, ritualized alignment of a latent higher awareness with body, breath, mind, and will. A properly cultivated inner guru becomes a silent companion who ensures one does not drift in chaos or sentiment, but moves forward with purpose and verticality.

A Tantric Approach to Time and Eternity

Consistent with Hindu metaphysics, Traditional Tantra views time as both cyclical and eternal. As Mircea Eliade explains in *Yoga: Immortality and Freedom*, cycles repeat endlessly in the cosmic order — Yugas follow one another, kalpas cycle, and even *Brahmā's* lifetime dissolves into regeneration after death of the world. Cyclic time operates as "wheels within wheels," implying concentric phases of both declining (involutionary) and ascending (evolutionary) currents within cosmic time.

Time as *māyā*, the cosmic illusion, ultimately carries a degenerative current — modernity's technological "progress" aside, which tends to revolve around comfort, convenience, and consumption. Such lower developments contribute to greater decline — social atavism, psychic confusion, moral dissolution — while giving an illusion of "advancement."

Yet alongside this cyclical decay exists a concept of eternity: *akṣara*, the timeless absolute. Tantra proposes that moments of spiritual intensity can evoke an eternal present, a paradoxical intersection of temporal and eternal — what Eliade calls the "lightning flash" of mythic time.

In *Ride the Tiger*, Evola outlines a strategy to survive and transcend the Kali Yuga without retreating from modern life. The dark age is compared to a tiger, and confronting it head-on ensures destruction while fleeing it yields defeat. A superior strategy is to "ride" the tiger — to operate within modernity, use its forces, yet remain sovereign: unmoved internally, aligned with eternal principles.

Evola's differentiated man retains apoliteia — an inner detachment — while acting where necessary, with courage and integrity. Such engagement mirrors a Tantric adept's challenge: to participate in mundane life without being ensnared by its illusions, and transform temporal action into vertical presence. Though one lives within time's webs, one no longer is of them.

A Tantric life accepts two realities. First, the profane wheel: time's cycles of formation and dissolution currently manifesting in social decay, psychic confusion, and spiritual hollowness. Second, a sacred now: eternity's timeless presence felt in rituals, consciousness, and moments of alignment (*in illo tempore*).

This dual awareness becomes a weaving of opposites. One stands amid modern chaos yet always in alignment with vertical order. Such awareness provides clarity when temporal currents turn chaotic, and confusion attempts to claim the mind.

Concretely, note how Yuga-based decay shows in fleeting trends, moral shifts, collective emotional outbursts — and how this pressures behavior. Yet, one may tune into the eternal — even if only during meditation, resonating with each mantra and breath. This becomes a daily tension of extremes, kinetic and reflective, conveying horizontal urgency and vertical stability.

A Practical Meditation: Visualizing Time and Eternity

This guided visualization cultivates a stance of sovereignty — the posture of a Tantric tower standing through time:

Preparation: Sit in a stable posture (e.g., *siddhāsana*), palms resting on knees. Steady the breath and calm your presence.

Visualize the Clock of Time: Imagine an enormous wheel overhead: the Yuga cycle, with golden Satya at the top, gradually darkening through Treta, Dvapara, to black Kali at the bottom. See ancillary wheels — societal, technological — that spin fast, promising illusory progress. Feel the pull of gravity downward toward decay and triviality.

Center the Eternal Point: Once this sense of descending cycles is vivid, imagine a still, brilliant point at your *ajñā* chakra (third eye). That is the eternal now (a timeless Self) anchored amidst all movement. Hold this point firm in awareness.

Breath through Time and Eternity: With each inhale, bring awareness outward to the spinning wheels. With each exhale, draw back into *illo tempore*. Repeat this action for four minutes. Afterward, recite, "I ride the tiger of time, but I am anchored in eternity — unbound by temporality, unbroken by decline."

Grounding: Complete this exercise taking a deep breath in and devoting presence to the day. Engage *mūla bandha* (contract perineum), pause, then release lock and breath. Rise mindfully.

This practice yields a felt awareness of decay as cosmic law, and yet not personal doom. It instills a felt vertical axis within, anchoring one to eternity amidst flux. It prompts a capacity to act in temporality informed by ageless insight. This is a resilient, non-reactive posture — to be of the world, but also past it.

This fulfills Evola's ideal: existing within time and beyond it. Not being naive to its structures, but unmoved by them. Engaged yet centered, acting from strength rather than fear.

Modern developments — knowledge, security, ease — can appear beneficial. However, a Tantric outlook discerns whether these changes encourage inner ascent, clarity, and self-mastery. Or do they dilute vitality, support reliance, and diminish drive?

Modern time is death-dealing when experienced as progress with no metaphysical context — the "terror of history" revisited daily. The practice proposed helps maintain discernment. Using modern tools without being used by them, living in time without being its prey: these are mindsets to cultivate.

Tantra teaches how to navigate time's tides by seeing them through eternity's lens. Evola's "tiger-rider" finds freedom not by escape but gaining mastery over time — by knowing its cycles and generating immunity to decay. Modernity's superficial advances obscure an essential atavism in its core regression to cruder, more profane ways.

In Evola's vision modernity is a mid-umbra of a temporal cycle. It is an age of spiritual eclipse, yet not total extinction. Living through it requires being a person of internal stability amid a collapsing world.

Juxtaposing cycles of time with moments of abiding awareness teaches how to transfigure conditions instead of fleeing them. Equipped with clarity, a differentiated man radiates vertical order from within. A practice of visualizing time and eternity ensures one's actions remain aligned with greater structure, immune to time's seductive decay, and waking the mythic form amid this historical void.

Through awareness practice, ritual methods echoing mythic time, and internal posture of sovereignty, one does not reject time but commands it. The true goal is to act within time yet from the center of eternity.

Thus, a Tantric approach to time and eternity is not escape — it is active detachment. It is knowing the temporal currents and swimming upstream through a still point within. One stays present: responding, creating, fulfilling earthly obligations while keeping the Sacred visible, alive, and at hand. That is the art of the Tantric warrior in these dark cycles. It is to ride the tiger, not perish under it; and in so doing preserve Tradition within oneself until the wheel turns again.

Integral Man and Absolute Realization

In Tantra, ritual initiation known as *dīkṣā* is regarded as a pivotal ceremony of spiritual ascent, preparing an aspirant to embody the Absolute (Shiva). According to Evola's *The Yoga of Power*, initiation remains crucial for awakening the internal spiritual force (*śakti*), reinforcing an awareness that spiritual power must be activated, not simply imagined.

This is a method for what we will call *Hautrī Dīkṣā*, organized around a fire ritual (*agnikārya*). This can be fulfilled either with a qualified guru or as a self-initiation performed solitarily by an aspirant. The sacrament is split into external, physical elements and internal, psychic activations. The outer hallows and confers; the inner awakens presence and resonance.

The goal of *dīkṣā* is making an aspirant into either a *siddha* or *jīvanmukta*. A *siddha* is someone who has fully mastered both inner and outer dimensions of Tantra, having dissolved all forms of energetic and mental bondage to life. A *jīvanmukta* is a person who has realized Self (*Brahman*) even as life continues. In Tantric language, this represents apotheosis: a grasp of deity within human form, merging Shiva (pure awareness) and Shakti (dynamic energy) into lived experience.

A realized being demonstrates absolute inner sovereignty, unshaken by external conditions. He exudes energetic mastery, guiding subtle currents at will; vitalized presence (*tejas*) and unfiltered clarity; spiritual action rooted in manifest existence. He is a unity of will, transcendence, and integrity, reflecting the archetype of a "differentiated man" who commands his own axis and stands as a force amid chaos.

Hautrī Dīkṣā Agnikārya

Purification (Śauca): The aspirant bathes in sacred water. The ritual space is cleansed. An altar is set facing northeast.

Construction of Kunda: A triangular fire pit (*kunda*) is built using bricks or stones. This serves as a focus for the initiation.

Saṅkalpa Declaration: The aspirant recites, "With reverent devotion I dedicate my life to awakening Shiva within me. May fire consume artifice; may my soul arise in cosmic power."

Opening Mantra: The aspirant thrice chants "*Oṁ Namaḥ Śivāya,*" connecting to Shiva and a higher frequency.

Kindling the Fire: Offer dried wood to the assembled fire. Invoke Agni as Shiva, reciting three times "*Oṁ Agnaye īśāna-rūpe Śivāya namaḥ.*"

Oblations (Ahutis): Using a spoon, pour four drops of clarified butter (*ghee*) into the flames while chanting the mantra: "*Oṁ Oṁ Draḍhī Śakti Oṁ.*" Each oblation represents an attribute: purity, strength, presence, and realization.

Pūrṇāhuti (Concluding Offering): With fixed intent, perform a final offering chanting the final mantra "*Oṁ Aḥ Śivāya*," sealing the ritual proper as complete.

Jñānavatī Dīkṣā — Internal Empowerment

Mantra Installation: Seated near the fire in a meditation posture, the aspirant intones a chosen mantra, focusing on the point between the eyebrows (*ajñā*): locus of realization.

Energy Sealing through Bandhas: Engage *mūla*, *uḍḍiyāna*, and *jālandhara* bandhas together with subtle breath retention. Visualize the Shiva yantra filling a subtle *bindu* at the crown.

Subtle Light Rising: Envision a rising shaft of light from pelvis to crown, energizing the *suṣumnā-nāḍī* and merging Shiva with Shakti in the body.

Kriyāvatī Dīkṣā — Outer Confirmation

Guru or Self-Performed Seal: If a guru is present, he invokes the mantra and places a hand near the disciple's *ajñā*. In self-initiation, an aspirant mimics this, placing a palm at the brow and intoning "*Oṁ Aham Śivāya Oṁ,*" closing the sacred space.

Circumambulation (Pradakṣiṇa): Perform three clockwise circles around the fire, each accompanied by the mantra "*Oṁ Śive Namah,*" integrating the cosmic energy field.

Gift of Mantra (Daṇḍa): In traditional rituals, the guru grants a mantra or instrument. In self-initiation, the aspirant establishes a silent intimacy with a mantra previously installed, resolving to obey and honor it.

Closing Ashes Offering: Sprinkle a pinch of the fire's cooled ashes on the crown of the head, symbolizing a consecration of body and consciousness as temples of Shiva.

Final Affirmation: Recite thrice "*Aham Śivāya Śivāham*" ("I am Shiva, Shiva is I"), asserting identification with the Absolute.

Grounding: Drink sanctified water and meditate in front of the waning fire, reflecting on unity of Self and sensory world.

Initiation is an act of spiritual aristocracy — structured, disciplined, fearless. By conducting ritual fire, mantra chanting, and self-sealing, an aspirant displays mastery not only of inner, but also outer form. Thus they become a vertical sovereign, embodying heroism fused with Tantric awakening.

This *Hautrī Dīkṣā* is a precise formula for realization where an aspirant passes into the realm of spiritual authority. Through fire, mantra, ritual form, internal sealing, and integration, an aspirant becomes a *siddha*, fully awakened and alive.

To receive this initiation is to choose sovereignty, awaken the centered Self, and live as Shiva in form. It is a ceremonial reinvestiture with cosmic truth and birth into a being that walks as one awakened among dreamers. This is a stage of spiritual development: not escape from life, but a change from within life by becoming a man of integral realization.

Vital Fluids and Retention

In Tantra, vital fluids — especially semen — are more than biological substances. They are energetic carriers of life capable of nourishing a subtle body (*sukṣma-śarīra*), fortifying mental resilience, and galvanizing spiritual potency. Mastery over these fluids is an act of energy transmutation central to sustaining *ojas*, the refined essence of vitality. This is about turning primal energies into refined spiritual fuel that aligns with a path of the warrior-spirit.

In Ayurvedic and Tantric thought, *ojas* is the finest distilled substance of all bodily tissues and energetic activity, closely connected with *kapha*. It circulates through the nerves and heart conferring immunity, clarity, emotional stability, and presence — hallmarks of a fully embodied subtle body.

It supports strong breath, mental steadiness, and spiritual receptivity. Without *ojas* vigor fades, emotional stability falters, health weakens, and spiritual faculties diminish.

In *Yoga: Immortality and Freedom*, Mircea Eliade underlines how the subtle body — our field of energy, emotion, and thought — is a true vehicle for spiritual ascension, outliving even the gross physical form.

Julius Evola's emphasis on transforming life's raw energies aligns precisely with this. Sexual potency is not to be sacrificed, but refined into subtle strength. *Ojas* is that substance which sustains *tejas* (radiance) and *prana* (life force), binding spiritual energy with a physical shell. *Ojas* is the fuel of a sovereign man, as opposed to an impotent "last man."

One of the most esoteric and mistaken Tantric practices is *Vajroli Mudra*. This is a refined technique designed to retain and redirect sexual fluids back into one's subtle energetic system. The *Shiva Samhita* calls it a "secret of secrets," recommending it even for a householder (*gṛhastha*).

This bears no resemblance to mere celibacy or simple semen retention. Instead, it combines pelvic muscle dexterity, breath control, subtle energetic locks, and mental focus to turn *retas* into spiritual essence. Its purpose is not sexual asceticism, but alchemy; preserving this vital juice not because sex is evil, but since the fluid carries potential for spiritual transformation.

The technique typically begins with asana and breath control, then proceeds to subtle contractions in the genitals: guiding energy up rather than out. When mastered, *Vajroli* redirects sexual secretions through the subtle central conduit (*vajra-nāḍī*) into higher chakras, enriching *ojas*, illuminating mind, and providing fuel for fire (*kundalinī*).

Practically, it helps overcome sexual dysfunction, manage urges, and maintain energetic sovereignty, even within marital or ritual sexuality.

Modern discourse often conflates *Vajroli* with simple semen retention or harsh celibacy. But Hatha texts clarify it as a complex technique involving precise control over muscle, breath, and subtle bodily systems. It is not sexual subdual, but a disciplined exercise in energetic skill.

Equating this practice with celibacy removes its technical potency. Adepts preserve vitality through conscious energetic training. Correctly performed, *Vajroli* permits continued sexual union and even non-ejaculatory orgasm while transmuting one's vital juice into spiritual *ojas*.

The modern environment encourages uninhibited release of libidinal energy through compulsive masturbation and habitual, unrestrained sex. In this context, men risk reducing themselves to Nietzsche's "last man" — a sterile caricature lacking strength, presence, and purpose.

Evola's counsel in *Ride the Tiger* is uncompromising: one must develop inner discipline, soar above herd impulses, and refuse emotional domestication. *Vajroli Mudra* becomes an act of heroic resistance — an assertive, sovereign exercise of sexual and spiritual will. Instead of leaking vital essence, one becomes a vessel of radical self-mastery, cultivating dignity and resolve amid a culture of degeneration.

The *Katha Upaniṣad* describes *ojas* as a refined outcome of sensory experience — one sustaining both mind and presence. Avalon's *Serpent Power* emphasizes subtle energy control as key to awakening *kundalinī*. Thus, *Vajroli* should be included in an effective Tantric repertoire, especially if practicing *maithuna*.

From an Evolian-Tantric perspective, vital fluid retention and *Vajroli Mudra* represent heroic acts of self-sovereignty. They are transformative technologies: practices engineered to preserve life force, sharpen will, awaken presence, and align everyday vitality with cosmic intent. In an age of dissolution, they prepare a practitioner to stand tall — energetically vibrant, emotionally centered, spiritually active — remaining rooted in poise, strength, and resolve.

Vajroli Mudra represents a refined practice within Tantric and Hatha traditions, crafted to transform sexual fluid into spiritual luminosity. Rather than suppressing energy, an adept undergoes a ritualized process of containment, redirection, and elevation. When performed skillfully it revitalizes *ojas*, deepens energetic clarity, and amplifies subtle-body presence.

At its core *Vajroli* depends on pelvic-floor mastery. The practitioner consciously contracts a pubococcygeus (PC) muscle, akin to an advanced Kegel exercise, sealing the urethral channel. Simultaneously, one applies *Mūla Bandha*, an energetic lift of pelvic center, and *Uḍḍiyāna Bandha*, the inward and upward abdominal draw. Through coordination, these bandhas build energetic pressure drawing semen upward through an energetic network, preventing its outward release. Precision is required: both muscular control and inner elasticity must coexist.

To retain fluid during intercourse, a practitioner pauses near climax and contracts the PC muscles, engaging the *Jālandhara Bandha* (chin-lock) alongside a gentle breath-retention. A light vacuum effect in the urethra assists inward drawing, while a practitioner visualizes fluid being transmuted upward through the *suṣumnā-nāḍī* toward the heart, then crown. This process gently accelerates *kundalinī's* advent and anchors awareness in refined vitality.

Mastery unfolds through patient engagement across five stages. First, an adept practices pelvic contractions daily. Over time, one refines sensation and nerve control. Second, these contractions are practiced during arousal without any attempt at fluid control.

Next, all three bandhas are combined with breath retention, deepening energetic integration. An adept then tests retainment during low-intensity arousal, discovering a subtle pull of the fluid inward without strain. Finally, an adept brings full Yogic precision into tantric intercourse, proceeding slowly, ritually, and consciously.

Supporting physical practices include core-strengthening asanas such as squats, cobra pose, and meditative circulation of energy through one's microcosmic orbit. Dietary moderation, consistent sleep patterns, and restorative breathwork reinforce a sustaining force of *ojas*, ensuring reserves for practice.

In ritualized intercourse (*Maithuna*), partners begin by synchronizing breath and intention. A deliberate pause near release transitions into bandha engagement and inward pull. Partners hold eye contact and breath, each supporting the other's energetic presence. After the fluid draws inward, both remain motionless, visualizing a shared flame ignited at the heart, sealed with spiritual fervor.

With consistent discipline, practitioners often feel warm energy flowing along the spine, deeper mental concentration, and an abiding sense of serenity. Sexual energy moves from a source of temptation to a reservoir of empowerment. Creativity and emotional balance strengthen, and the practitioner gains an ability to embody clarity in everyday interactions.

Vajroli is not a casual skill — it demands humility, subtlety, and ritual integrity. The adept must proceed gradually to avoid upsetting physiological or emotional equilibrium. If a teacher is available guidance is recommended, though self-practice can be valid if approached conscientiously, with awareness that intense energetic shifts should be tempered with introspection, physical grounding, and emotional attunement.

Vajroli Mudra is not just a sexual skill; it is a sophisticated energetic procedure weaving together bodily discipline and vital awareness to transform sexual force into spiritual dynamism. Practiced with patience and intent, *Vajroli* becomes medicine for the will — a method to forge presence, strength, and grace amid instable currents of modern existence. It serves as a track on which practitioners may anchor their verticality, illuminate their purposeful existence, and discover transcendence in the very substance of life.

Being mastery is not easy nor fast, *Vajroli* is best embraced with respect and careful training. Its reward, however, can be profound: a subtle awakening that hones both power and presence, inviting a practitioner to stand tall as an unwavering axis within their world.

Pelvic Muscle Coordination

Sit comfortably (cross-legged or on a cushion). Contract the PC muscle (perineal floor), pulling tightly toward the spine. Hold for 8–12 seconds, release, and repeat 12-24 times. This builds the muscular awareness required for precise control.

Applying the Bandhas

Mūla Bandha: Engage the PC muscle, lifting energy upward.

Uḍḍiyāna Bandha: On exhaling, draw the navel inward and upward beneath the ribcage, creating abdominal suction.

Jālandhara Bandha: Tuck the chin to the chest to seal the throat and stabilize internal pressure.

Coordinating all three during breath retention forms the energetic conduit for drawing fluid upward.

Vital Fluid Preservation

During sexual activity approach the point before ejaculation. Pause movement, engage bandhas, and tighten the PC muscle firmly. With relaxed breathing, apply pressure as if drawing fluid inward. This must be gentle, controlled, and synchronized with sensation.

Visualization for Energy Flow

Mentally trace the semen's pathway from the perineum into the sacral chakra, then upward through the spine into the heart and crown. Imagine a warm, glowing white current ascending with each inhalation.

Foundational Retention Training

Stage One — Basic Pelvic Strength: Daily, perform a round of 12-24 PC contractions interspersed with holds. Integrate into routines (e.g., holding during traffic lights).

Stage Two — Bandha Integration: Begin by applying *Mūla Bandha* alone for an 8-second hold. Add *Uḍḍiyāna Bandha* while exhaling, then release slowly. Later, add *Jālandhara Bandha* — coordinating all in succession. Perform 4-8 bandha cycles daily.

Stage Three — Dry Retention Practice: In arousal, contract PC and hold, focusing on upward sensation. If fluid approaches release, pull back, tighten, hold, and breathe calmly.

Stage Four — Controlled Fluid Retainment: During minimal sexual stimulation, pause at the ejaculatory threshold. Utilize tightening, inward draw, and bandhas to retain fluid. Start slow, gradually increasing retention skill and hold duration.

Stage Five — Maithuna Skill: With a supportive partner, engage in Tantric intercourse. Pause near climax, lock bandhas, apply draw, and visualize upward flow. Hold 4-8 breath cycles, release gently, and resume a slow, intentional movement.

Partner Practice — Ritualized Maithuna

Sacred Orientation: Create a simple altar with a surface, candle, incense, and devotional symbol(s). Sit in a position called *Viparita-Maithuna* (man sits in *padmāsana* or like pose; woman enters his lap, wrapping her legs around him) — also known in Buddhist *Vajrayana* as *Yab-Yum* — and synchronize breathing.

Invocational Mantra: Recite together, "*Om Namah Shivaya, Oṁ Hrīṁ Śrīṁ Klim*" three times to infuse sacred intention.

Engage Slowly: Begin intimate contact. Before either reaches climax, the male partner contracts PC and locks bandhas. The female mirrors this by contracting her pelvic floor, providing energetic reciprocity.

Retention and Visualization: Hold still, maintain pressure, and circulate energy upward. Sustain for 4–8 breaths in a state of full, silent awareness. Uncouple and face the altar.

Closure with Mahāmudrā: Seal energy by sitting with legs extended, spine straight, chin tucked, and hands in Dhyana or on knees. Hold for 2–4 minutes, then end chanting, "*Om.*"

Vajroli Mudra is a methodical and potent technique weaving together somatic discipline, breath mastery, focused intention, and ritual structure. When practiced with care and reverence, it unlocks sexual energy as a vehicle for spiritual empowerment. It likewise turns intimacy into an act of presence, power, and transcendence.

Through diligence and ritual, practitioners forge a subtle, yet powerful alchemy. Sexual energy is not lost but transmuted. Every ritual union becomes a step on the path toward authentic spiritual realization.

Greater Maithuna Rituals

In Traditional Tantra, sexual rites (*maithuna*) represent an apex of transforming opposites into divine union. Mircea Eliade, in *Yoga: Immortality and Freedom*, describes how sexual union becomes ritualized, embodying Shiva (consciousness) and Shakti (energy) as cosmic principles. In the *Kularnava Tantra*, sexual union is explicitly mythologized: "The true sexual union is the union of the supreme Shakti with the Spirit (*Ātman*); other unions represent only carnal relations..." *Maithuna* is also a profound act of worship — the merging of divine polarities.

Evola's *The Yoga of Power* clarifies that these rituals are not indulgences, but magical techniques requiring strict discipline, mastery, and transcending the egoic. They are called "initiatory sexual magic," wherein release is transformed into subtle energy and union becomes transcendental.

Monthly Greater Maithuna Ritual for Couples

Couples committed to a full tantric discipline may undertake a monthly greater maithuna — a formal, full sexual ritual with boundaries and intent. This ritual is a culmination of devoted partnership, systematic alignment, and mutual transformation. The sexual ritual is a sacred act, not ceremonial erotica.

Designed to be performed once per lunar cycle at the full moon, the ritual begins with mutual purification — physically cleansing and ritually consecrating both the space and the participants — signifying a removal of commonplace domestic patterns. Invocation of Shiva and Shakti via *nyāsa* is an act of harnessing raw archetypal energy; each partner invites a cosmic polarity into their subtle body.

Synchronized breathing, bandhas, and mantras act as a conduit for raising *kundalinī* energy. These transfer sexual force into subtle channels rather than dissipating it. Together, they create a shared energy field pointing toward transcendence.

The retention of sexual fluid builds heat (tapas), subtly consolidating inner force. Closure through *mahāmudrā* and silent meditation is critical — it crystallizes the energy into a subtle shape conducive to ongoing spiritual integration. The ritual concludes with grounding, stillness, and reflections in a shared journal, affirming that the act was not indulgence but a shared journey into deeper awareness.

Preparation: The couple purifies bodily and environmental space: bathe, don sacred garments, adorn with flowers, burn incense. They set a *saṅkalpa* such as: "Through us let Shiva unite with Shakti in an embrace that births the cosmos."

Nyāsa and Mantra Installation: Each partner invokes and seats the Other within their subtle body. The man touches points (crown, heart, navel) intoning "*Oṁ Namaḥ Śivāya,*" and the woman likewise recites "*Oṁ Hṛīṁ Śrīṁ Kḷīṁ.*" This act identifies them as cosmic half-lotus vessels in union.

Tantric Embrace: The man sits in *padmāsana* or a similar posture; the woman enters his lap in *Viparita-Maithuna* (*Yab-Yum*), legs wrapped around his waist, embodying unity. The posture is stationary, maintaining stillness as subtle energies exchange without physical stimulation.

Breath, Bandha, and Sound: Partners synchronize breath — mutual *prāṇāyāma* — engaging the *mūla* and *uḍḍiyāna bandhas* to control energy flow. They recite "*Om,*" aligning breath with sound vibrations, transforming arousal and sexual stimulation into spiritual ascent.

Visualization: Each partner visualizes a *kundalinī* serpent uncoiling, ascending through *sūṣumṇā-nāḍī*, penetrating chakras, and ultimately merging their subtle flames in the *bindu*. Thus, the sexual energy becomes a conduit to cosmic union.

Retention and Union: Skillfully controlled, the male's semen is preserved and sublimated into subtle channels as sacrament (*brahmavandha*). Partners then sit in *āsana* facing each other.

Closure with Mahāmudrā: After shared stillness, partners seal energy using *mahāmudrā*, with spine erect, chin tucked, and breathing and awareness elevated. Follow with the mantra "*Om,*" each anchoring individual presence within a communal ritual field. Engage in shared meditation through gaze.

Integration and Journaling: After rising, walk in silence to ground the energy. Journaling impressions and insights serves as a ritual of witness and self-inquiry — tracking subtle clues of personal transformation.

Annual Grand Maithuna Group Ritual for Paired Couples

An annual grand *maithuna* gathers multiple couples in a discreet, ceremony-rich event intended to amplify collective energy through sacred symmetry and shared intent. The ritual elevates partnership to a communal act, acknowledging that a collective of awakened individuals can embody a more extensive field of cosmic polarity.

Designed to take place in a ceremonial space with multiple couples, this rite expands the energetic architecture. The circle, pensively lit and solemnly prepared, aligns all participants in symbolic geometry — each couple is both an individuated duo and a node in a larger Tantric matrix. A shared *saṅkalpa* shifts focus from personal transcendence to a collective awakening, transforming the ritual into a group act of layered devotion.

As each couple enters *Viparita-Maithuna* posture, the energy transforms into a resonant field of awakened polarity, vibrating with amplified force. Simultaneous breath, *bandha*, and *mantra* unify participants across the circle, conjoining personal release into a ritual grid of shared energy. Retention is imperative, as it prevents energy from dispersing, instead channeling it into this shared energetic space, and ultimately the spiritual plane.

After a thorough cycle, participants close with *mahāmudrā* and attend to collective grounding. This is a vital step to prevent energetic dissipation and emotional dissociation.

Sacred Circle and Preparation: Participants purify jointly, lighting lamps at a central altar that contains both a Sri Yantra and Shiva-Shakti iconography. All observe silence and a shared *saṅkalpa* of cosmic communion and spiritual expansion.

Structured Seating: Couples sit equidistantly in a circle and face toward the altar. A ritual leader and fully authorized initiate opens with mantras "*Oṁ Namaḥ Śivāya*" and "*Oṁ Hrīṁ Śrīṁ Klīṁ,*" installing collective energy into the field.

Mutual Invocation and Nyāsa: Each couple conducts *nyāsa* separately, focusing into the center and aligning subtle bodies with a group field. Silence and concentration maintain cohesion.

Simultaneous Maithuna Union: At the leader's guidance, all couples assume *Viparita-Maithuna*. Breath is synchronized and bandhas (*mūla* and *uḍḍiyāna*) are activated in unison.

Expanded Sound Mantra: Together, the group chants thrice "*Om Hroum Namah Shri Mata Shaktyai.*" Attention is shared for a duration 2-4 minutes to build shared subtle resonance.

Collective Visualization: Couples visualize their individual *kundalinī* rising and merging at a central celestial *bindu*. They imagine being nodes in an energetic cosmos, echoing Avalon's description of chakras as microcosms of planetary energies.

Controlled Retention and Energy Flow: Seminal retention remains central; orgasm is transmuted into subtle fire. Couples maintain union until the leader signals a shared recitation of "*Om.*" This consolidates energy within the circle.

Mahāmudrā: Participants then sit in *āsana* facing the center. All perform *mahāmudrā* in unison, silent for 2-4 minutes as the energy field integrates. The leader signals another shared "*Om.*"

Dedication and Gracing: The leader then offers a dedication by blessing the circle, energy, participants, and cosmos. Prayers may articulate intent and foster discipline, courage, and clarity in spiritual hearts and everyday living.

Closure, Grounding, Silence: The ritual ends by snuffing the central flame. Participants walk outward in silence.

Evola sees these rituals neither as carnal indulgence nor superficial devotion, but disciplines requiring full mastery. He emphasizes sexual energy must be retained, structured, and sublimated producing *ojas*. Lost semen equals death of energy; controlled, it becomes inner fuel activating spiritual power.

Only through ritual can physiology be transformed into spirituality. Matters of *kundalinī*, chakras, and subtle flux apply directly: maithuna is a catalyst that activates the latent serpent, coiling into awakened consciousness. Woodroffe, in *Introduction to Tantra Śāstra*, insists on ceremonial purity, sacred gestures, and authorized structure without which sexuality remains merely carnal.

These rituals require preparation through daily *sādhanā*: *asana*, *bandha*, *prāṇāyāma*, *mantra*, *yantra* practice. Discipline fosters readiness. So too does right conduct — chastity outside ritual, emotional integrity, and mental clarity.

Regular journaling allows tracking of internal and relational effects: subtle shifts in awareness, inner strength, emotional stability. Silence and witnessing (one's inner guru) are central, emphasizing responsibility and reflection.

Couples must maintain mutual discipline and reverence. These rites demand shared intent, trust, and the restraint of release until energy is deliberately transmuted. Monthly rituals refine skills; the annual ritual anchors collective force.

Participants may experience a heightened psychoenergetic power, deeper unity, sharpened intuition, and greater presence beyond such rituals. The sexual act is never an end in itself; it instead exists as a tool of transformation. It is a fire through which consciousness is tested, tempered, and ennobled.

Maithuna rituals are practices of magical action wherein sex becomes a means of transformation. Through disciplined practice these rites enhance inner power, aligning the psyche with subtle cosmology to evoke presence within existence. They reveal sexuality as both a crucible of spiritual sovereignty and catalyst for sacred union.

Over time, these rituals become touchstones for broader transformation. The energetic union forged ripples into daily life: partners experience enhanced clarity, mutual empathy, attunement, and emotional stability. Participants often find that relationships outside ritual shift.

When conducted with mastery, sexuality is reshaped into sovereignty. Rituals are weapons of spiritual warfare. They are disciplined, elevated assertions of order amid degeneracy.

Tantra of the Black Sun

Shiva is usually adorned with a crescent moon, symbolizing his lunar traits — calm, intuitive, and magnetic. Yet this imagery reduces him to a lesser, subordinate celestial body, reflecting an inversion undermining his cosmic primacy. Conversely, Avalon describes Shiva's bindu as "the silent source of all forms and energies," occupying an apex of spiritual realization.

Unlike a center of planetary systems, the moon orbits Earth. Symbolically, this makes Shiva subservient to a feminine telluric presence; a configuration reinforcing a gynocentric dominance within mainstream Tantra. Evola warns against such reversals, since they erode a Traditional hierarchy. This is a crucial bearing for a spiritual warrior who must stand unyielding amid decline.

Astronomy places a supermassive black hole at the galaxy's heart. It is an immovable, all-consuming gravitational center around which systems revolve. In Tantric lore Shiva is called *Mahākāla*, the "Great Time" that dissolves all form.

In this sense, reimagining Shiva as a "Black Sun" asserts his primacy as an obscure center around which all revolves. Rather than orbiting, he holds all in his gravity — also operating as a portal to the beyond. He exists as a mysterious midpoint, rather than some glowing satellite.

This realignment affirms Shiva's role as "Unmoved Mover," root of both creation and destruction: transcendent, eternal, and sovereign. In this reframing, Shakti's terrestrial counter is the clear receptive polarity. Her energy draws from Shiva's center; she remains formidable as the Tantric Earth Mother, but never overriding Source. This alignment preserves divine hierarchy, reestablishing a masculine authority at Tantra's heart while still honoring the divine feminine.

Vedic and Tantric traditions distinguish the fierce destroyer Rudra from Shiva, divine absolute — yet also acknowledge their ultimate identity. In this schema, Rudra can be viewed as Shiva's expressive force: destruction through power radiating from the Black Sun. Rudra operates outwardly within the cosmic field while Shiva remains a fixed center. This resolves ambiguities and restores unity through coherence.

The *Nasadiya Sūkta* from the *Rig Veda* opens with cosmic origin in impenetrable darkness, rising from silent heat — not lunar calm but primordial gravity: "Darkness there was at first... That One by force of heat came into being..." In the Upanishadic tradition, *Shiva-Mahākāla* remains beyond creation, the timeless core in an ocean of form. Avalon sees Tantric ritual as ascending toward Shiva's bindu, the silent root of all energy.

Evola encourages the formation of an inner gravity-field of presence — a personal axis that remains unmoved amid modern decay, analogous to a Black Sun at the center of one's being. Woodroffe states ritual is intended to align consciousness with absolute centers, not ethereal cosmologies.

Subordinate symbolism enervates the masculine archetype, reducing spiritual warriors to orbiters around external poles. Recasting Shiva as Black Sun restores vertical authority and centers spiritual practice upon the silent, gravitational core of consciousness that is sovereign posture.

A Shaivite of the Black Sun acts from centralized awareness — a spiritual gravity-field — with energy and ritual orbiting around that center. Such postural calibration echoes Evola's notion of differentiated manhood, where one stands unmoved and sovereign within the haste and decay of modernity.

The Black Sun paradigm corrects the Tao inverted by lunar symbolism and restores cosmic and spiritual integrity. Shiva is center of our galaxy, while Shakti remains vital but subordinate, and Rudra serves a dynamic function of change emanating from the core. Ritual, meditation, and sexual transmutation practices become gravitational alignments rather than revolving gestures.

For the Tantric practitioner, this model offers both cosmic metaphor and internal technology, aligning ancient edifices with fresh metaphysics. It creates a vertical orientation essential for enduring sovereignty and spiritual freedom in an age of decline. It is a true Tantra of the Black Sun.

On WarYoga

From the view of Traditionalist metaphysics, the pursuit of a Shaivite Tantric spiritual regimen represents one of the few viable paths for transcendence in the Kali Yuga. In his seminal work *Yoga of Power*, Evola elucidates Tantra as a virile, heroic path of overcoming rooted in a dynamic interplay of Shiva (the transcendent, immutable principle of pure consciousness) and Shakti (immanent, creative force of energy and manifestation).

Tantra, particularly in its *Kaula* and *Vāmācāra* (left-hand) variants, demands an adept harness the body's latent power (sexual, vital, and somatic) to awaken *kundalinī*, dissolve illusions, and achieve a state of divine sovereignty. Yet, as Evola warns in *Ride the Tiger*, modernity assaults a differentiated individual with its leveling forces, eroding the inner fortress required for such work. To fortify it, one must enhance Tantra with a rigorous and assertive physical discipline — and an ideal fitness appendage is outlined in *WarYoga* by Tom Billinge.

This integration is highly complementary, being based in practices drawn from ancient Indo-European physical culture. The first book in particular details India's *vyayam* system based out of its Akharas (sacred gyms). WarYoga's exercises transform one into a true "warrior of the spirit" capable of embodying the solar, imperial ethos of primordial Tradition.

As the "Lord of Beasts" (*Pashupati*) and destroyer of illusion, Shiva embodies a static pole of eternity while Shakti, his consort, animates the flux of becoming. This path is perilous for the uninitiated, as it risks devolution into mere hedonism if not grounded in a warrior's discipline. Likewise, in the Kali Yuga the body's vitality is sapped by modern toxins (processed foods, sedentary life, and psychic pollution) rendering it unfit for such physical alchemical operations.

Here, WarYoga intervenes as somatic armor, drawing from Vedic origins where yoga was born amid heroic striving and a pursuit of power. Explicitly a protest against the modern world, WarYoga's worldview aligns with Evola's call in *Ride the Tiger* for a spiritual aristocrat to detach from bourgeois conformity, cultivating an inner sovereignty that expresses itself outwardly as physical prowess through disciplines like *vyayam*.

Billinge's WarYoga system revives an ancient synthesis of physical exertion in a yogic context, tracing it to Indo-European roots where rhythmic movement was an austerity generating inner heat (*tapas)* for spiritual ascent. The text posits WarYogic practice as a "striving for higher states of consciousness... set against the background of war, heroism, cattle raiding, and the pursuit of power," resonating with the claim in *Yoga of Power* that true Tantra is martial, not pacifist.

The staple physical regimen in WarYoga comprises rhythmic exercises: *ḍaṇḍs* (push-ups), *beṭhaks* (squats), *sūrya namaskār* (sun salutations), *gada* (mace swinging), *joṛī* (club swinging), and *mallakhamb* (pole gymnastics). All are performed in an *akhara* under patronage of *Hanumān*, the heroic avatar of Shiva.

These are not ordinary calisthenics, but alchemical tools. As Billinge describes, they build a "body of one colour" (uniform, radiant physique). This is done via an internalized sacrifice, mirroring the Vedic *ātmayajña* (self-sacrifice) where the body becomes one's altar and exertion their ritual.

This complements Tantra by providing a virile foundation. The adept's body, tempered like Indra's *vajra* (thunderbolt), becomes a vessel for *Śakti's* ascent without fracturing under *kuṇḍalinī's* force. In *Yoga of Power*, Evola praises such somatic masteries as essential for haṭha yoga's "violent" methods. They force one's *nāḍīs* (energy channels) open through physical rigor, preventing the psychic imbalances plaguing modern seekers.

The complementarity is most evident in *vyayam's* emphasis on *tapas*, *prāṇāyāma*, and *rasa* (essential fluids), which Billinge links to *Siddhi* alchemy — the Tantric quest for immortality. *Tapas*, the "heat of austerity," is generated through repetitive *vyayam* movements, akin to a friction of churning the cosmic ocean in myths where *Śiva* drinks poison to birth *amṛta* (nectar). Drawing upon Tantric texts, this is the heroic path (*vīra-mārga*) where a body is subjected to ordeals to awaken latent powers.

In WarYoga, exercises like *ḍaṇḍs* and *beṭhaks* build explosive strength and resilience at the core of the regimen, externalizing a microcosmic *dharma yuddha* (righteous war) of inner combat against dissolution. Per Billinge, a *vyayam* specialist embodies Indra's delight in power, rejoicing in body while transcending it, much like a Tantric *vīra* who uses eros without attachment. This solar masculinity — unyielding, central, ordering — is required to sustain a Traditional metaphysics of sex.

Vyayam cultivates this through its solar symbolism. *Sūrya namaskār* yokes a practitioner to *Savitṛ* (the solar deity), aligning with the identification of Śiva as an esoteric sun beyond physical manifestation. Billinge notes how the *sūrya namaskār* integrates aspects of *vyayam* with *yoga āsanas*, representing a formal synthesis echoing basic movements of *ḍaṇḍs* and *beṭhaks*, fostering both physical strength and muscular prowess essential for Tantric endurance.

Moreover, WarYoga's *brahmacarya* (continence) and dietary regimen — emphasizing sattvic foods like kurak (a nutrient-dense mix) and avoiding modern poisons — bolsters Tantric *maithuna*. Billinge notes *vyayam* practitioners conserve *bindu* (seminal essence) to fuel inner fire, a direct parallel to Evola's metaphysics in *Eros*. Semen is not wasted but transformed into *ojas* (vital radiance), enabling one to "ride the tiger" of sexual energy without being destroyed by it. In the Kali Yuga, an aristocrat of soul must practice "active impassivity," engaging the world from a detached place — *vyayam* provides this.

As Billinge notes regarding the "yogic body," the rhythmic swinging of a *gada* induces a meditative state, stilling one's mind amid repetitive motion. This "stillness in physicality" complements Tantric *dhāraṇā* (concentration), where an adept holds *mudrās* during union to bind *Śakti*. Without such physical anchoring, Tantra risks devolving into New Age indulgence; with WarYoga, it becomes a forge for the Siddha: a refined being who abides outside cosmic cycles.

As the most iconic *vyayam* tool, a *gada* strengthens spirit and body, building grip intelligence, shoulder mobility, and hip drive through rhythmic swings that unify the body's movement. Billinge depicts it as a symbol of discipline and self-governance, connecting a practitioner to ancient forebears and yoking the divine within the tool to the *ātman*.

This synthesis evokes a primordial Indo-European warrior: the Marut storm-god, yokemate of Indra who Billinge identifies as the WarYogin archetype. Tantra traces to Vedic sources where *Rudra-Śiva* is a wild ascetic whose dance (*tāṇḍava*) destroys and recreates. Supplementing Shaivite sadhana with *vyayam* revives this: an adept becomes a "child of the light" yoking body to sun through practices like *samtola*.

Against modernity's afflictions this path offers liberation. As Evola urges in *Ride the Tiger*, a differentiated man must "detach from the human" to reclaim divinity; WarYoga's akhara is the training ground for this, where sweat is oblation and victory is self-sovereignty. This is attained in exercises like *joṛī* swinging, which builds tremendous forearm, wrist, shoulder, and neck strength while churning vital fluids akin to milk.

To delve deeper, consider Evola's critique in *Yoga of Power* of diluted yoga. Modern *āsana* lacks the virile intensity of Tantra's "secret way." WarYoga restores this through *vyayam's* ethical code. *Yama* and *niyama* are interpreted specifically as disciplined austerities, which align with a Tantric *vīra's* devotion to humility, courage, and devotion.

Drawing from Atreya and Alter, Billinge's text posits *vyayam* as "more yogic than most modern yoga," stressing excellence via sensory control through mechanical repetition that transforms food's dynamic energy into stored potential. This links to sacred eros: an oiled body in *vyayam* evokes a Vedic sacrifice, where oil (*rasa*) is a fluid oblation. This is a Tantric parallel to using sexual fluids for *amṛta* production.

The *mallakhamb*, though less common, sustains heaven and earth like the *Skambha* (axis mundi). It allows one to ascend the world tree through leg grips, jumps, and yogic postures. These enhance flexibility and core strength, aiding in attainment of *āsanas* in Yogic and Tantric practices.

WarYoga's historical lineage (from Vedic origins to Maratha revival) mirrors a Traditional narrative where cycles of decay are countered by heroic revivals. The *vyayam* routine of waking pre-dawn and practicing tapas prepares one for Tantric effort, ensuring *Śakti* flows unimpeded. Heavy tools like *gada* and *joṛī* build a “majestic body” typifying a solar ideal. This is a physique radiating inner beauty; one immune to modernity's snares.

In *Yoga of Power*, Evola cites the *Haṭhayogapradīpikā's* call for a strong body to contain *kuṇḍalinī*. WarYoga provides this crucible. WarYoga’s rhythmic exertion simulates *Śiva's* conquest of demons.

Billinge's *ātmayajña* (internalized sacrifice) parallels Tantric *pañca-makāra* (five M's) rituals, which work upon the principle of transmuting flesh into spirit. For a spiritual aristocrat this is essential. Riding the tiger means harnessing *Śakti's* fury through action-based practices like *vyayam*, achieving *jīvanmukti* (living liberation) as divinity awakened to its true nature.

Fully embrace this path by forging your body through the trials of effort. Awaken *Śakti* in Tantra's embrace, and likewise fortify Shiva through WarYoga's patron Hanuman. Ascend the throne of the Lord of the World through *ḍaṇḍs*, *beṭhaks*, *gada* swings, and *mallakhamb* ascents.

Ultimately, Tantric union empowers a seeker to embody the Axis Mundi — *Skambha*, the upright *liṅga* — where stillness meets motion. Going beyond that, a Tantric WarYogin rises as Indra, smashing illusion with vajric strength forged in *vyayam*. WarYoga is the hammer and anvil; Tantra is fuel and flame.

"Fight the Inner War. Become a WarYogin." —Tom Billinge

Nietzschean Affirmation and Riding the Tiger

Nietzschean affirmation refers to the radical acceptance of existence in its entirety — embracing joy and suffering, health and defeat — as intrinsically valuable. As Heidegger observes, the philosopher's idea of eternal recurrence requires affirming "what is and will be" in a hard, determined cosmos, and then overcoming it with a "nameless freedom." Nietzsche criticizes life-negating cynicism like Schopenhauer's as an anemic form of spiritual pessimism, advocating instead a vigorous *"yes"* to life. Despite our Kali Yuga's acute failings, this affirmation means accepting the entire journey of life willingly and even joyfully.

In *Ride the Tiger*, Evola adopts Nietzsche's stance toward nihilism and chaos, advising us to utilize modernity rather than struggle or flee from it. The tiger symbolizes unruly, dangerous, looming power. Facing it head-on invites annihilation, and recoil tempts defeat. Instead, one must mount it — with mastery, restraint, and clarity — to guide its movement and harness its potency. This is Nietzschean affirmation in practice: engaging in ostensibly "degenerate" behaviors without being lowered by them, and instead harnessing them for upward mobility.

Evola defines this strategy as "a transition from the plane of 'Dionysus' to that of a spiritual superiority, known ... as the Apollonian or Olympian symbol." This course avoids regression and rejects resignation. It is affirmation as spiritual action.

Consciousness can shape reality through ritual discipline, breathwork, mudras, energetic optimization, and ascesis. These disciplines spiritually reflect Nietzsche's *will to power*, a force that shapes the inner world to confront the outer. Tantra's mix of charged symbols, *kundalinī* dynamism, and sexual spirituality parallels Nietzschean self-overcoming: both insist raw force be mastered in form and sublimated by acts of will.

In Tantra, an aspirant channels powerful vital energy — expressed in the *kundalinī* serpent — through discipline, not denial. Similarly, a Nietzschean channels life's energies to shape himself. Both turn chaotic potency into sovereign form.

Since *Ride the Tiger* was published, cultural and moral ruin has furthered. Technology destroys cognizance, relationships are reduced to consumption, and established family structures vanish. Traditional forms continue to dissolve. The moment therefore demands more: the joy in travail, a clear-eyed realism, and an anchor of ritual sovereignty have never been more vital.

Romantic love may often be misguided or broken, but it can be made sacred if imbued with vows, ritual, and reverence. Love rooted in duty and transformation can elevate partners — instead of codependency or possessiveness is a shared spiritual purpose. Likewise, sex becomes a numinous union instead of an instinctual drive, a pleasurable escape, or even just lovemaking.

Young men must take up the task of affirming life, claiming their axis, and riding the tiger. Romance need not be weakness; it can become the stage for sacred possibility. Sovereign conduct isn't about domination, so much as command — of oneself. It is foremost one's access to optimal energy, awareness, and form.

The modern world profanes every area of life, but one must still engage it with sacred intent. Do not hate the tiger or fear it: *ride it.* Let this challenge become your path to mastery. Achieve excellence using chaos as your crucible; its subdual your trial.

Let your life be a triumph, not submission. In every breath, every utterance, every moment: *affirm.* You are not a last man, but one differentiated — warrior, lover, magician, master.

ॐ त्र्यंबकं यजामहे सुगंधिं पुष्टिवर्धनम्।

उर्वारुकमिव बन्धनान् मृत्योर्मुक्षीय माऽमृतात्॥

Om Tryambakaṃ yajāmahe sugandhiṃ puṣṭi-vardhanam
urvārukam iva bandhanān mṛtyor mukṣīya mā'mṛtāt

"We worship the Three-Eyed One (Shiva), who is fragrant and who nourishes all beings. May He liberate us from the bondage of death, like the ripe cucumber is freed from the vine, but not from immortality."

—Ṛigveda

www.ingramcontent.com/pod-product-compliance
Lightning Source LLC
LaVergne TN
LVHW051559080426
835510LV00020B/3052
* 9 7 8 1 9 6 8 3 9 4 0 2 8 *